Dividend Investing

A Complete Step-by-Step Beginners Guide to Dominate the Stock Market and Build Your Own Passive Income Toward Financial Freedom with Investing in Dividend Stocks

Andrew Stock

Table of Contents

Introduction

Welcome to Dividend Investing: *A Complete Step-by-Step Beginners Guide to Dominate the Stock Market and Build your Own Passive Income Toward Financial Freedom with Investing in Dividend Stocks.* By choosing this book, you've chosen to give yourself a guide to financial success through the dividend market.

Within this guide, you'll find practical advice on learning how to recognize trends in the market, reinvest your funds, and choose between stocks that are on the rise and those on the downturn. You'll learn about dividend trading from the ground up, starting with basic terminology, reading stock charts and graphs, and understanding how dividend trading works on a small and large scale. You'll also learn research skills, what metrics to look for when choosing dividend stocks, and about ways to save and spend your dividend income to maximize your financial freedom.

When you've completed this guide, you should be aware of the income and tax implications of dividend trading, and how to build a portfolio to best take advantage of your income opportunities while maintaining an affordable tax bracket. You'll be able to identify the pros and cons of dividend trading, the differences and similarities between dividend trading, and other forms of brokering, and you'll know a good stock from a bad stock when you see it. You'll even learn valuable information about the history of the stock market and how to use that knowledge to read the market in the present and the future.

Dividend Investing: *A Complete Step-by-Step Beginners Guide to Dominate the Stock Market and Build your Own Passive Income toward the Financial Freedom with Investing in Dividend Stocks* is meant to take the guesswork out of getting started with investing, reinvesting, and building a solid income through dividend trading. The detailed information in this guide should serve as both a starting point and a reference for you, as you move into the world of dividend trading.

The internet has brought the ability to trade to the fingertips of anyone with a computer or smart device. Gone are the days of needing expensive stockbrokers and trading houses buried in mounds of ticker tape. Let this guide take you from start to finish through all the basics you need to get started, on your own, with dividend investing and passive income. When we're done, you'll be ready to jump into the world of dividend trading, armed with research skills and real-world knowledge.

With so much to do, let's get started and begin to reap the dividends!

Chapter 1: What is Dividend Trading?

For someone who may have never invested before, the terminology can be a bit confusing. Dividend trading is only one form of trading, and it is important to know exactly what you're getting into before you get started. Being a successful dividend trader requires that you be well-versed in a few crucial elements, and learning the terms and definitions surrounding the practice of dividend trading is a great place to begin.

What does it All Mean?

Dividends are the payments given to stockholders, either in the form of a cash payout or additional stock shares. In essence, a company pays its stockholders simply for owning its stock. These are often paid out quarterly or monthly depending on the company. In the United States, dividend payouts are most usually aligned with quarterly reports, which are required by law. Some companies choose to pay out dividends once or twice a year, and some are completely irregular.

The amount of a dividend is a portion of the company's earnings per stock multiplied by how many shares you own. For example, if a company was going to pay out a one-dollar annual dividend, it might choose to pay out twenty-five cents each quarter. For every share you own, you'll receive $.25 each quarter. For a thousand shares, you'd get a quarterly check of

$250. This might not seem like much, but over the course of a year, you'd receive a full thousand dollars. If you owned a dozen similar stocks, you could bank or reinvest $12,000.

When a company is preparing to pay out dividends, there are four very important dates accompanying the payout. The first date is the *declaration date*. This is the day that a company's board of directors or other leadership 'declares' that they will be paying out a dividend. Once the declaration is made, the company is now liable for paying the dividend.

Two more important dates accompany the declaration date: the *date of the record*, and the *payment date*. The date of record is the day that the company will determine who its shareholders are and will review its records up to that date. The payment date is the day the payouts will be made.

The fourth date and the most important is the *ex-dividend date*. This is the last day that shares can be purchased to receive a dividend payout once the declaration is made. It is almost always two business days before the date of record. If you purchase shares in a company after the ex-dividend date, the previous owner of those shares will be the owner of a record and will be the recipient of the dividend payout.

Another important term to learn about dividends is *dividend yield*. The dividend yield is a calculation of the relationship between a company's average annual dividend payout and its stock price. The dividend yield is a constantly changing number, based on the fluctuation of the stock's price over the course of the trading day.

$$Dividend\ Yield = \frac{Annual\ Dividend}{Current\ Stock\ Price}$$

-How to calculate dividend yield-

The dividend yield can be calculated using the above formula. If a stock price is at $100, and the annual dividend is $2 a share, then the dividend yield would be $0.02 or 2 percent.

High-yield dividends are those stocks that have a high yield percentage. These can be enticing because the potential for income is greater, but it is important to examine why the yield is so high. In some cases, it's because the stock price has fallen, affecting the yield ratio. If that's the case, you should take a good look at the stock itself before purchasing it for dividend income.

In other cases, the yield is high because the company offering shares may not be one which needs to pay income tax on the stocks - this could be something like a master partnership or a real estate holding company. We'll talk more about tax implications later in this book, but for now, it is just important to know that these types of high-yield dividends require the recipient to pay the income tax on them, lowering the actual amount you'll receive.

Some Other Important Terms

When getting involved in trading, whether it be for dividend investing or otherwise, it's crucial to have a basic understanding of the terminology commonly used in regard to the stock market. Below is a short glossary to get you started:

Annual report: This is information that companies put out each year to try and draw new investors and keep their current investors apprised of the company's status. It will include things like earnings reports, new products, or services on the horizon, and give an overview of the company's finances and accomplishments.

Bear market/bull market: A market that's trending on the rise is known as a "bull market," and a market that's trending downward is called a "bear market." These terms are often used by finance reporters and stock and fund brokers to determine whether it is a good time to trade.

Beta: This is a measurement of a stock's volatility against the market itself. The market is given a value of 1.0, and stocks which track higher than the market over time have a higher beta, and those that trend lower than the market over time have lower beta.

Blue chip stocks: These are the stocks of large, well-established companies and corporations that often have a stable dividend payout and are unlikely to have large swings in yield.

Buy/sell: The act of purchasing or ridding oneself of stock shares. This can be done all in one day, known as day trading, or through limit orders designed to buy or sell a stock or number of stocks once the shares reach a previously determined price.

IPO: This is the "initial public offering" of a stock when the company decides to be publicly traded. Depending on the success of the IPO, more shares may be issued in a secondary and tertiary offering.

Moving average: This the price of a stock over a certain period of time, most commonly 50 or 200 days. The moving average can tell you a lot about the stability of a stock.

Portfolio: This is your total collection of investments, including all your stocks, bonds, and trading funds.

Sector: This is a group of companies in the same industry as technology or travel. Comparing stocks in a specific sector can give you an idea of how that industry is faring.

Spread: This is the difference between the asking price and the bidding offer on a stock. For instance, if a buyer wants to purchase a stock for $10 a share, but the seller is asking for $12, the spread is $2.

Stock symbol: This is the one-, two-, three-, or four-letter abbreviation used in the markets for each company that is publicly traded. For example, communications giant AT&T is denoted as simply the letter "T," while Home Depot is "HD," 3M is "MMM," and Microsoft is "MSFT."

Trading Volume: This is the number of stock shares sold during a trading day. This is a good indicator of the stock's value and stability.

Volatility: This is how quickly a stock price moves up and down. Stocks that stay relatively stable have low volatility and those with prices that fluctuate greatly have high volatility.

By familiarizing yourself with these terms, you'll be that much closer to understanding the way stocks are traded. If it feels a bit like learning a foreign language, that's okay; like any language, the more you use it, the more fluent you'll be.

What Sets Dividend Trading Apart?

There are many different methods for making money on the stock market, and dividend trading is just one way to assure yourself some income through investing. Just what makes dividend investing so different?

In dividend investing, you're not only looking for a stock that can make you money as it is traded but a stock that will also pay you just for owning it. Not all stocks pay dividends, and often, newer companies will not offer dividends. This is because these companies are using their income to pay back into growing the business rather than paying stockholders.

There's also a bit of a myth that dividend trading or investing is only for older traders looking to pad their retirement income. While dividend investing is very suitable for this purpose, in recent years, many people have turned to dividend investing to build a nest egg or to establish college funds, make large purchases, and have more flexibility in their careers by not relying on a sole source of income.

While ordinary, or regular, dividend income is subject to being taxed at regular income tax rates, dividends that fall under the criteria of 'qualified', are also taxable but at the lower capital gains rate. This is important to keep in mind when you are choosing dividend stocks in which to invest. While it's also important to keep a diverse profile, you may want to consider investing in such a way to ensure qualified dividends. You want to be able to pay the lower tax rate on your earnings. We'll talk much more about how to make your dividends qualified in later chapters.

When you diversify your portfolio, you can consider things like investing in growth stocks, which focuses on making money quickly from stocks on a rising market, or investments like mutual funds, where a group of investors goes in together (mutually) on a portfolio of stocks and bonds. There are also ETFs, which are electronically-traded funds similar to a more traditional mutual fund. There's also any number of treasury bonds, which offer a secure, long-term investment but do not offer much growth.

While practices like day trading or purchasing growth stocks can offer a quick turnaround on investment, traditional dividend trading is geared more toward long-term growth. For shorter-term trading, options like capital investing, purchasing IPO stocks, and day trading may be for you. In the next chapter, we'll discuss the pros and cons of dividend investing, so you can decide if it is a strong investment strategy for you.

Chapter 2: The Advantages and Disadvantages of Dividend Trading

There are distinct advantages and disadvantages to all types of investing, and dividend trading is no different. The stock market has never been a guaranteed method of earning income, and while dividend trading is a more stable form of investing, that doesn't make it foolproof. Let's go over those pros and cons to help you make a more informed decision about whether or not dividend trading is a method that would be beneficial to your portfolio.

The Upside of Dividend Trading

There are several true advantages to investing in dividend stocks, not the least of which is the ability to grow your investment and raise your personal profits. When you invest in dividends, you are lowering your market risk in purchasing that stock. Once a company announces dividends, even if the price of the stock falls drastically, you will still be the recipient of a return on your investment.

If the stock price rises after the declaration date, you will not only make a profit on your shares, but the dividend yield will also increase. By investing in dividend stocks, you've taken some of the gambling out of the stock market. There is also a very good chance that the company you've invested in will increase their dividend percentage as time goes by. Most of the large corporations and blue chip stocks have steadily increased their dividend payout every year for a number of years.

Since the early 20th century, nearly half of all income made on the stock market has been earned from dividends. Many investors find that dividend investing yields a higher profit than long-term bonds or mutual funds. The return on dividends is often higher than the interest rate on other types of investments.

Another benefit of dividends is that examining them can provide you with a good indicator of how healthy a company is. Looking at an annual report will give you an overview, but those reports are geared to make a company look its best. By using long-term dividend yield or looking at average return on investment, you'll get an idea of how well that company's stocks have done over time and can make a more informed decision about buying those particular shares.

Dividend stocks also tend to have less market volatility, which can make them a very stable part of your investment portfolio. If you lose money on the stock price, its dividend could make up for the loss, leaving you at net zero. Dividend stocks also tend to fare better in a bear market, because they are offered by established companies and corporations who are less likely to be greatly affected by market swings. Even in the Great

Recession of 2008, dividend stocks remained much more stable than non-dividend stocks.

The tax advantages of dividend-paying stocks are also not to be trivialized. Regular dividends are taxed at your standard income tax rate, but qualified dividends are taxed at the much lower capital gains rate and can even be tax-free in certain circumstances.

In America, qualified dividends are those which are offered by corporations based in the United States and have met requirements set by the Internal Revenue Service (IRS). The second requirement of a qualified dividend is that you must own it for a certain period of time (for example, 60 days of a 121-day quarter). More on that in the chapter on tax implications!

Another advantage of purchasing dividend stocks is that the dividend payouts also tend to outpace the rate of inflation. That means that your dividends will provide income greater than the devaluation of the currency, which also increases your profits as well as your reinvestment and purchasing power. Being able to reinvest your dividend income back into the market is a great way to ensure that your dividends increase steadily over time.

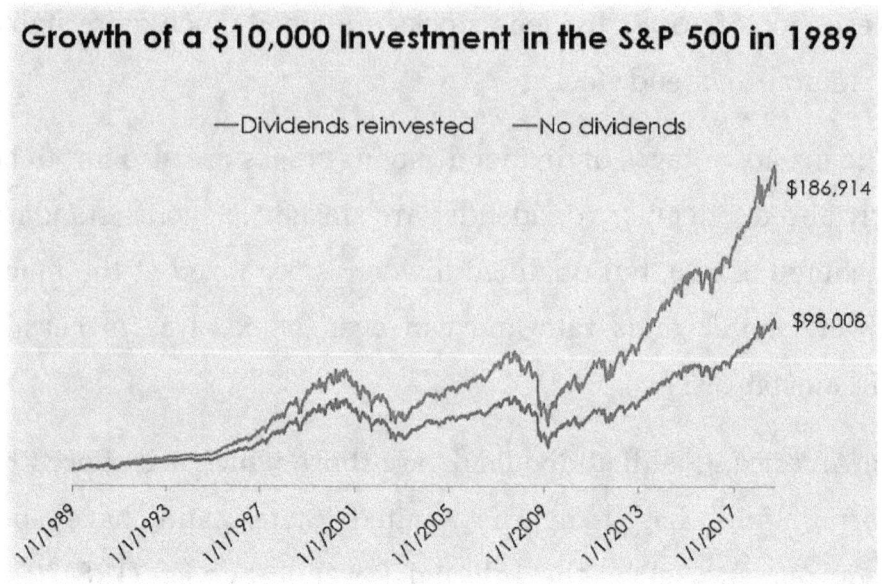

Growth of a $10,000 Investment in the S&P 500 in 1989

—Dividends reinvested   —No dividends

$186,914

$98,008

- Dividend stock income/reinvestment v. non-dividend stock income over 18 years-

The Downside to Dividend Trading

While the advantages of investing in dividends can make it a very attractive option for your portfolio, you should be aware that there are some counterpoints to consider before diving into dividend stocks.

One of the first things to be aware of is that companies do not have to pay dividends on their stocks, and in fact, many do not. But just because you purchased stock with the expectation of receiving dividends, does not mean that payout is guaranteed. Publicly traded companies are only bound to paying dividends once they've made a declaration. If no declaration is made, no dividend is paid. Companies that historically paid dividends could stop at any time.

Another thing to take into consideration when purchasing dividend stocks is the pace at which you can make your income. If you are taking risks in the stock market to try to make a large amount of money in a short period of time, then dividend stocks may not be the best investment for you. Because of their stability and generally low volatility, dividend stocks tend to have a lower beta and slower pace of income from the stock itself.

You should also be vigilant about watching the interest rates on the stock market, which are regulated by the Federal Reserve Board, or 'the Fed'. The Fed is the United States' central banking system, and one of its main functions is to adjust long-term interest rates to alleviate or avoid financial crises. The Fed mandates policies that help control inflation and deflation by keeping watch over the nation's monetary supply.

If the Fed adjusts interest rates, not only are the rates on things like long-term loans or mortgages affected, but the stock market is affected as well. This is because investors are always looking for the best return on their money, and if interest rates are low, people have more money to spend. Interest rates will influence whether or not investors choose to put their capital into things like CDs (certificates of deposit), real estate, or the stock market.

When interest rates are low, consumers have more financial freedom, but when interest rates are high, spending becomes tighter. It's important to be aware of how the interest rates affect the consumer spending market before making any investments in the stock market, even in stable stocks like dividends. High-interest rates can cause stock prices to fall because both consumers and businesses will cut back on spending.

As interest rates go up, dividend stocks tend to underperform in the market because investors become less interested and less willing to make longer-term investments. It is crucial to look at the interest rates to look ahead to see what the Fed is expected to do each quarter and to monitor your own portfolio for stocks which could be affected by rising interest rates. Despite their stability, dividend stocks shouldn't be a case of 'set it and forget it.' They need to be evaluated and reevaluated just like any other stock.

Interest rates aren't the only rates that should be monitored. You'll also want to look at tax rates because dividend stocks are taxed at regular income tax rates, and qualified dividends are paid at lower rates. But tax rates can change any time, and you'll also need to be aware if your dividend income is going to put you into a different tax bracket. With tax laws seemingly changing every year, you might want to consider retaining the services of a qualified tax accountant or certified public accountant when you enter into the world of dividend trading.

Not to get too personal, but your age can also affect whether or not purchasing dividend stocks is the right investment strategy for you. On one hand, investing in dividends when you are young is a stable, low-risk way to begin building a retirement nest egg. On the other hand, if you are trying to build your initial personal wealth, you might want to consider growth stocks or other forms of higher-risk, higher-yield investing.

Because it can take a long time to build savings using dividend stocks, and the income is not always guaranteed, you'll need to be cognizant and consistent in how you invest your money in dividend stocks. Think about all the large corporations of the last two decades alone that have gone out of business - companies like Radio Shack or Toys'R'Us. Those companies consistently paid dividends, but in the end, their bankruptcy and subsequent insolvency may have left inattentive investors out in the cold.

One last thing to consider about the potential disadvantages of investing in dividend stocks is also one of the things that make them so relatively stable. Often, there is not much diversity in dividend stocks. The companies that offer dividends and paying out to their shareholders are not reinvesting that money into research and development. If companies are not reinvesting in themselves, there may not be much potential for growth.

Many dividend stocks are from old businesses, ones that have been operating under the same or similar business model for decades, maybe even more than a century. They may be utilities or manufacturers that specialize in one range of products and services, or they may not be representative of an industry that experiences much change.

No matter the reason, dividends can be an indicator that a business is using its earnings to pay their investors rather than reinvesting the money back into the business. While the dividend payout is obviously a good thing from the investors' standpoint, it is important to look at each company as a whole and be able to determine their long-term stability and viability before investing in their dividend stocks. Because of the seeming lack of diversity in dividend stocks, you may want to make sure you have diversity in other parts of your investment portfolio. Don't miss out on great opportunities by focusing solely on one form of investment!

Once you've mulled over the advantages and disadvantages of dividend investing, and you've decided that this investment practice is right for you, it's time to think about how you're going to go about adding dividend stocks to your portfolio. In the next few chapters, we'll examine how to plan your portfolio, choose the right stocks for you, and how to avoid some of the most common mistakes that new investors make when building their investments.

Chapter 3: Making a Practical Plan for Investing

Rare would be the person who knows nothing about the stock market and who is still able to make money. Buying and selling stocks comes with its own risks, its own language, and its own set of (sometimes very complex) rules, but when done correctly, it can be extremely profitable and rewarding. Most people wouldn't buy a house without securing a mortgage first, and investing in dividend stocks is a similar potentially long-term investment.

Find and Define Your Funding

Once you've decided to take the leap into investing in dividend funds, you need to know how you are going to purchase them. It is impossible to do anything in our capitalist society without, you guessed it, the capital. Will you be relying on personal savings to start your investment portfolio? Are you considering using money from other investments, such as a mature bond? It's crucial to know the source of your capital before you begin purchasing any dividend stocks.

The other vital element in finding and defining your funding is determining how much you'd like to invest- and sticking with it! Because investing in any stock, even in those that pay dividends, comes with inherent risk, it is crucial to be aware of and comfortable with the amount you are willing to spend on your initial investment. Much like a gambler going to a casino, you have to know your limits and be able to cut your losses when necessary. It's easy to throw good money after bad, but being sure to have a budget and staying with it will lend some discipline in your stock spending.

If you will be borrowing money to make investments, you'll want to make sure that the interest rate on your loan isn't going to preclude the profit you could potentially make from your stock income. This is also not the preferred method for financing your stock portfolio, because the risk inherent in trading stocks could mean you lose your capital before you can repay your loan. It is best to have more secure forms of funding when investing in the stock market.

You should also keep your 'market money' separate from your other funds. This isn't only because you want to make sure you keep on budget, but because it will make things like reinvesting or preparing your taxes easier in the long run. By leaving your stock finances separate, you'll reduce the temptation to spend the money on other things, save yourself time and money when it comes to tax time, and know where your portfolio stands at a moment's notice.

Dividend stocks, like most stocks, vary in price, but once you've done your research into the types of shares you'd like to buy, you can begin crafting a financing plan that will fit your budget and get you started on the path to purchasing the stocks that are right for you. Remember, the entire point of dividend investing is to build an income, not lose savings. You want to live within your investing means when you first get started, and then you can begin spending more as your income allows. It is not worth going above your resources; investing should be an exciting prospect, not one that causes you undue mental and financial stress before you've even gotten started!

Get Started on Stock Research

If you are unfamiliar with buying stocks, it can seem like a daunting task to choose the ones that will fit into your starter budget and give you the income you are looking to bring in. The wonderful thing about living in the era of technology is that the internet holds a wealth of information right at your fingertips. Being able to research nearly any company and any stock whenever you'd like is a valuable tool to have at your disposal. The best advantage you can give yourself is to be a strong researcher.

In the past, anyone wishing to invest in the stock market would have to employ the services of a stockbroker, many of whom were shysters who would take advantage of uninformed clients. With the resources available to you through the internet, you can do enough research to decide if you'd like to use a broker or go through the investment process yourself on an e-trading platform. You can even use one of the many available 'robo advisors'- automated brokerage systems which can help you decide on stocks through data analysis and market trends.

When you're ready to begin your research, there are a couple of different methods you can use. If you're completely unfamiliar with investing in the stock market, you should find a good finance website and 'market watch' for a week or two. Familiarize yourself with the rise and fall of the markets each day and learn how to read the charts and graphs. Another way to begin learning all the language is to watch investing shows and videos. YouTube holds a wealth of investing channels, and there are entire cable and satellite channels devoted to finance. There are even podcasts that address the subject.

In short, you want to be comfortable with the terminology and the process of trading before you begin. To really dive into the stock market, there's no such thing as too much research. You can brainstorm a list of companies that you think you'd like to purchase shares of, and then look up each company, read their annual report, and see how their dividends pay out. Or you can search for lists of top dividend yields and then choose to research the ones on the list that appeal to you.

How much research you do is up to you, but it is important to be aware that the stock market is a fickle mistress. Anything could change at any time based on the mood of investors and business owners, what the interest rates are doing, and how certain industries are faring. You cannot be too prepared. You have to keep in mind that the market changes every day, despite dividend stocks being among the most stable. You want to research your stocks with all the fervor of a young child on a scavenger hunt and all the discipline of a scientist working on a Nobel prize-worthy discovery. In other words, be curious and passionate, but also diligent and exacting.

Open	107.67	Market Cap	580.5B
Prev Close	106.73	P/E Ratio (ttm)	12.56
Bid	107.70 x 100	Beta	1.38
Ask	107.75 x 300	Volume	24,551,265
Day's Range	106.82 - 108.00	Avg Vol (3m)	32,180,656
52wk Range	89.47 - 123.82	Dividend & Yield	2.28 (2.15%)
1y Target Est	124.11	Earnings Date	Oct 25, 2016 - Oct 31, 2016

-A sample daily stock report-

The Value of Annual Reports

Companies want you to purchase their stocks, and so they will take all the positive information they can muster to prove to you how much of a value their shares are, and why you should invest RIGHT NOW! The truth is, not too many corporations are as shiny and magnificent as they would have you believe in their annual reports because if it seems to be too good to be true, it probably is.

That being said, there is real value to be found in annual reports. They contain a large amount of information which you can use to make informed investments; you just need to know how to unwrap the facts. Annual reports of all publicly traded businesses have been required by the Securities and Exchange Commission (SEC) since the middle of the 1930s. These reports must include a description of the company's industry, products, and/or services. They must also include financial statements, cash flow, and income. The report will also contain a list of the company's board of directors and other leaders and what they've accomplished in the last year.

The part that should interest you the most is the stock valuation and dividend payout. Here's where you need to be able to fight through the fluff. Many companies will make their annual report into a propaganda piece, filled with juicy tidbits about research and development and colorful photos of happy employees enjoying lunch on a bench in the parklike setting outside the company's headquarters. The dividend payout list is in there somewhere, you just need to dig it out.

When you're doing research, it pays to get as much information as you can about a stock before you purchase anything. If you can, talk to other people who've invested in dividend stocks and get their feedback. If you can afford to have a consultation with a broker or financial planner, even if you plan on doing your own trading, you should take advantage of their expertise to help you get started. Don't be afraid to ask a ton of questions.

Not asking the right questions now could cost you money in the long run.

Because the internet is such a powerful research tool and there are opinions and analyses running rampant, do some searching. You'll find a diverse array of stock reviews, top ten lists, advice columns, investment blogs, and other articles on the topics you're curious about. You can search a single stock and get several different opinions on it, so make a list of the key points of each argument and see if the totality swings in favor of or against the stock you were interested in. We're not saying that every internet stock pundit is correct, but by analyzing their reviews and using your judgment, you can get a good idea of how the market is feeling about a particular stock at any given time. We'll talk much more about reading the mood of the market later in Chapter 6.

Make Your List and Check It Twice

If you know anything about carpentry or building materials, you'll have heard the adage 'measure twice, cut once.' You want to make sure that you've made the right measurements before wasting time and materials, and when it comes to purchasing stock, you want to ensure that you are putting your investment dollars in the right place before you spend them.

By the time you've done your initial research and narrowed down your list of desirable stocks, you've probably got a good idea of how those stocks perform. Before you go ahead and invest, take a little time to observe the market. Search for daily news on those companies to see in anything is developing that could drastically affect their market price. This could be new products or services being released, or new industry regulations. In other words, be an information sponge before and after you've decided to buy.

Because one of the advantages of dividend stocks is that they are so stable, you can afford to bide your time purchasing them. Chances are good that not much will change with those companies in the short-term, but it's always better to be safe than sorry. Check your data, and then find another source and check it again. As we've said, you can never do too much research.

Choosing a Trading Mechanism

Once you've secured your financing, set a budget, done your research, and decided on what stocks you'd like to begin your dividend investing journey with, it is time to decide how you want to purchase your stocks. Are you going to use a broker, an automated system, or an online trading platform? Let's take a look at the different ways you can manage your stock purchases and the pros and cons of each.

If you decide to use a brokerage service or financial planner, you should do some more research to find a broker or service that fits your needs and your budget. Brokerage fees vary widely and are based on industry standards, experience, and track record. The more experience your broker, the more you may have to pay for their services. This may seem like a flat-out downside, but if their experience can make you more money in the long run, it may be worth it.

Brokers also have access to data and research you may not be able to find publicly. If you choose to set up a brokerage account, you've already completed one part of the financial planning we previously discussed- keeping your market money away from your other assets. Experienced brokers will also be able to offer you advice and their insight on what stocks would best fit your objectives.

If you're more comfortable going with one of the big conglomerate brokerage firms based on name recognition, then, by all means, use them. Maybe you are more comfortable finding a local independent broker or financial planner. However, you choose to find a broker, be sure to do your due diligence and find one that has a track record of excellent customer service. You also want to be able to reach your broker when you have an urgent question or request, so be sure to research availability.

One other thing to consider when selecting a broker is the age and experience of the company. You want to find a brokerage that employs brokers and planners that are mature and well-educated, but also willing to be up on all the latest technology available for stock trading today. In this rapidly changing world, you want to know that you have both experience and adaptability in your corner. Technology plays an incomparable, irreplaceable role in the modern world, and the stock market is no exception.

While brokers are being paid by you to provide you as service, keep in mind that they are almost always working on commission, and they are salespeople. Treat them as such. While they should always have your best interests at heart, they are still trying to make money for themselves and move up the ladder at the brokerage firm. Be sure you do your own research in addition to any information they give you.

If a broker suggests buying a certain stock, be sure they can give you a solid, plausible reason why. It doesn't have to be a complicated answer, as long as it satisfies your need to know. Be sure you understand any advice that a broker gives you, and don't be afraid to say 'no'- you are the one paying for a service. Make sure that once the broker begins investing for you that you monitor the account activity closely.

There is also a big difference between full-service and discount brokers. Full-service brokers are what we've been discussing, and they are more expensive and offer more services than a discount broker. Discount brokers usually do nothing but buy and sell for you on your orders. As the name implies, they cost less to employ and usually require less money to open a brokerage account, but you get what you pay for. Before using a discount broker, make sure you fully understand the scope and limitations of their services. If you feel you'll need more advice than a discount broker can give, especially getting started with investing, you should consider a full-service broker, if only until you get your feet wet.

If you want to be semi-autonomous in your investing, you could use a robo advisor, of which there are plenty. Many brokerage firms and large investment banks have added this type of online service in recent years. A robo advisor is an automated system that recommends stock and bond investments based on a set of criteria that you input. That could include setting spending limits, identifying what type of sectors you're looking to invest in, or what stocks you'd like to avoid.

The advantage of this type of service is that it costs less money than a human advisor or broker but conversely cannot offer advice borne from human experience. You can try out a robo advisor using a relatively small amount of start-up capital, and see if the service is right for you. Talk to other people who use a robo advisor and get their feedback. When choosing a robo advisor, be sure you understand all the transaction fees, any commissions that you may incur, and how the platform works *before* making any trades.

One thing that may steer you clear of robo advisors is that they are generally used for more diversified trading rather than just dividend stocks. If that's the only thing you're interested in trading, you may find it better to use a full-service or discount broker, or just do your homework and do all the trading yourself through a trading platform.

There are definitely some people who feel more comfortable doing the work themselves, and if you're one of them, that's great! There is a wealth of online trading platforms available to you to manage your own account. These e-brokers provide a place to store your brokerage account, do research, and trade at your will nearly 24 hours a day from anywhere in the world. Sounds wonderful, right?

The truth is, these platforms are terrific and offer modern conveniences in trading that the founding fathers of the stock exchange could have never dreamed of. But they do still cost money, and they don't come with the human advice and experience of a full-service broker. If you think that you need that sort of guidance, at least until you get your feet under you, then a self-trading platform may not be for you.

When you're looking at an e-trading platform, you want to look at the services it provides and what it doesn't. Prioritize what's important to you, and choose a platform that best suits your needs. You should look at the minimum amount needed to open an account, the trading platforms' track records for security and ease of use, and what they take out for commissions. You should also research what their transaction fees are and look into their customer service offerings. You want to choose an electronic trading platform that is user-friendly and reasonably priced while fulfilling your needs as a client.

If you think that you may want to start with a full-service broker and eventually transition into doing your own trading, you can look for a brokerage firm that offers a mix of trading options, so you can begin by working with a broker and wean yourself off, as it were, without having to move your brokerage account. That will give you the peace of mind of having one less thing to do, as well as leaving you with the option to go back to using the full broker, should you need or want to do so.

By being both flexible with your trading mechanisms and aware of your own knowledge and limitations, you can begin to craft a trading strategy that will be effective not only for dividend trading but also for other investments, should you choose to build a diverse portfolio. The key points to remember are to be smart about your funding, know your spending limits, and don't be afraid to ask for answers and advice. Take advantage of all the resources available to you.

Once you've laid out all your funding and feel that you've completed enough research, it's time to actually start purchasing your dividend stocks. In the next chapter, we'll look at strategies and tips for choosing the best dividend stocks and making the most of your buying power.

Chapter 4: Tips and Strategies for Building Your Portfolio

Dividend stocks are a staple investment in any trader's portfolio, and even though we've already gone over how to get started with dividend stocks, you may still be wondering how to choose the best ones for you. In the last chapter, we discussed funding and research, and in the following pages, we'll delve a little deeper into how to do the best fact-finding, how to trade to your personality, and how to maximize your investment dollars when purchasing dividend funds.

Be a Stock Detective

We cannot emphasize enough the vital nature of research when you want to purchase stocks, especially for the first time investor. You absolutely cannot have too much information about any stock. In this chapter, we're going to go over a lot of information and give you some more new terms, but more importantly, how to put it all together to make sure you craft a portfolio that is diverse, productive, and manageable. The only way to reach your investment goals is by being a knowledgeable researcher who remains engaged in your own portfolio. We're going to show you how to begin that research and get on the way to attaining those goals.

When you first dive into your stock research, you'll want to find a way to track the stocks you're interested in and organize your information. If you're the pen and pencil type, a ledger notebook or graph paper can help you keep columns of data neat and accessible. If you're more computer-oriented, you can use a spreadsheet program like Excel to keep track of your research. Organize your data however you feel comfortable being able to go back and study it. You may find that as you gain experience, you'll begin to tweak your record keeping, but for now, choose a method to get you started.

You'll also want to find a daily finance website that you're comfortable with reading so that you can sign up to track the stocks you're interested in. Many of these sites are available, from Yahoo! to Google, to the Dow Jones page itself. Find the site that seems the most user-friendly to your tastes, and as you investigate each stock, you'll see that there's a button on most pages to 'follow' or 'track' a stock. Some sites even offer you a daily email or newsletter with that day's results for the stocks you've chosen.

When you first get started, you'll be looking at the obvious statistics like earnings and dividend yield, but which metrics can tell you the true story of a stock's performance? And once you've read them, how do you put them together to get an accurate picture of the stock as a whole? Experts say there are some key data points you'll want to examine before purchasing any dividend stocks, so let's look at some definitions and connections.

The first of these metrics is what's known as the *P/E* or price-to-earnings ratio. This number indicates the value of a stock compared to its earnings per share. Only companies that are making a profit will have a P/E ratio, so that's your first clue that a company is making money. The higher the P/E, the more growth the stock is experiencing.

When you look at a company's P/E ratio, you should be looking at past data and projections, because you want to get a clear picture of performance over time and what the future could potentially hold. Sometimes, a high P/E can indicate that a stock is overvalued, but to confirm or debunk that, you should look at the P/E ratios for other companies within the same sector. If they are all performing at similar P/E rates, that could be an indicator of accelerated growth within that industry.

What you want to see when you examine a company's P/E is a steady or growing ratio that will indicate the health of that business. If you see that a P/E ratio is on the decline, with no market or industry explanation, you may want to steer clear of that particular stock, at least for a while. If it is something you had your heart set on, you can monitor the stock for a while until you see if the P/E ratio improves or not.

Another metric you should take a close look at when researching dividend stocks is called *D/E,* or debt-to-equity ratio. This number, put simply, can help you learn how a company is leveraging its money. The ratio is calculated by dividing the company's total liabilities by its shareholder equity. The D/E can determine the company's ability to stay solvent should there be a sudden economic downturn.

The D/E itself or the figures needed to calculate D/E can be found on a company's balance sheet, which should be included in their quarterly and/or annual reports. You can find online templates for calculating it yourself if it is not immediately reported in those documents. High D/E ratios are often an indicator of high risk because it means a company is willing to go into a larger amount of debt to finance its growth. That doesn't necessarily mean that the stock is not worth investing in, but you should be aware of this and compare it with all the other metrics before making a decision about purchasing.

As you look at key metrics for dividend stocks, you'll obviously want to take time to study *dividend growth*. This is the data that will show you the value of a company's dividends over time, meaning rather than looking at the current size if the dividend, you'll be looking at the rate at which it has been growing. If you see steady growth that could indicate that the company is healthy and is willing to pay its stockholders in kind.

If you see a decline in dividend growth, you should examine what's going on with the surrounding market, sector, and company itself. Has there been a general downturn causing the company to need to hold more capital to stay solvent? Has the company recently announced a new product or service that they need to finance? A change in dividend growth is not negative or a positive until it is put into context, so be sure to examine what's going on around the market before writing off a good stock for slow dividend growth.

Another metric to consider strongly is that of *total return*. The total return is the amount a stock pays out on dividend plus the income earned through the stock price itself. For example, if a stock experiences a 10 percent market increase and pays out a 5 percent dividend, the total return is 15 percent. Stocks that routinely perform in this manner can provide a great deal of income, sometimes, in a relatively short period of time.

One last detailed metric you should take a look at when deciding on which dividend stocks to buy is *free cash flow*. This is the amount of money a company has left to spend after accounting for all its capital expenditures. Free cash flow, or FCF, can be used to fund growth or research, pay dividends, or put aside or reinvested. A company that not only has a great deal of free cash flow but also has a history of *stable, steady* free cash flow is probably a very good dividend stock investment.

Stable free cash flow means that a company is working with a business model that doesn't cause rapid fluctuations in assets and liabilities. While every company may, at some point, have an upswing or downturn, those businesses who are not living beyond their means with debts or liabilities will always have a free cash flow of some sort. These businesses know the importance of being able to use purchasing power even in times of financial regress.

There are so many ways to look at stocks and the metrics indicating their performance, but these data points will get you well on your way to understanding what's really behind the dividend numbers. But while numbers are crucial to choosing stocks, it's also important to purchase stocks that you find interesting. In the next section, we'll talk about how to buy stocks that fit your lifestyle, your personality, and your tastes.

Finding Stocks to Fall in Love With

When you are looking for stocks to invest in, especially dividend stocks that you may be keeping in your portfolio for a while, it is important to not only purchase stocks that will help you meet your investing goals, but also stocks that are interesting to you. If you think your portfolio is ho-hum, you're more likely to 'set it and forget it'. By purchasing stocks in companies and sectors that match your personality, you're much more apt to be an active participant in overseeing your investments.

For example, if you are a person who really enjoys travel, look for stocks from travel gear companies. You will enjoy following along with the company's stock but also learning new insights on the company's products. Investors often get a peek as to what lies ahead for the companies they invest in, and sometimes, there are other perks. These could be annual stockholder gatherings or advance deals on gear or experiences.

You can also choose to invest in companies that keep in line with your personal values or beliefs. If you are passionate about animal welfare, you could choose to only purchase stock in companies that support that value, such as cosmetic companies that don't participate in animal testing. You could also invest according to your religious beliefs, supporting companies that are Halal if you are Muslim, for example.

It's also okay to pick a stock just because you like a company. Seriously. Your grandfather likely had a few stocks in Standard Oil or Coca-Cola just to say he owned them. So go ahead and buy a little Nike or Pepsi or whatever sparks your fancy. Playing the stock market is a serious matter, but remember, it is your money to do as you wish. If owning a little piece of your favorite brand makes you happy and earns you a little income, then why not go ahead and buy it?

You could also consider investing in stocks from sectors you don't know much about, but would like to. If you're not much of a technology person, researching and investing in the tech sector is a great way to learn about products and services. By choosing stocks that keep you on your toes, you'll be more engaged in managing your portfolio and reading up on the companies you've invested in. Be careful, though. Most advisors or brokers would tell you to only invest in what you know, so if you are just learning an industry, don't get in over your head.

Get your feet wet and take time to learn about that sector until you can actually swim.

The bottom line is that even though dividend stocks tend to be a stable, low-risk investment, they don't have to be boring. By choosing stocks from interesting companies that make interesting products, you can build a portfolio you'll want to be a part of, rather than a passive observer. Your stock portfolio should be a source of income, but it should also be a reflection of you, your personality, your goals, and your interests.

Getting the Most for Your Money

When all the research is done and you've chosen the stocks you want to purchase, how can you buy what you want and get the most value for your investment dollar? This is where all your research comes into play. Because you must be the owner of the record for dividend stocks to receive the dividend payout, it falls to common sense that the actual 'when' to buy is before the ex-dividend date.

But 'when' should you buy, price-wise? If you are willing to sacrifice your first dividend payout in the short-term for the long-term gain, you could purchase your dividend stocks after the ex-dividend date, because the prices are generally lower +/- the dividend per share right before the dividend payout. Of course, this means the seller would receive this payout period's dividend, but also means that you'll be the owner of the record for the entirety of the next period. That means you'll likely own the stock long enough for it to be a qualified dividend, and you'll get taxed at the lower capital gains rate on the dividend.

To recap: To make a long-term gain with a short-term loss, purchase your stock right after the ex-dividend date when the prices are generally slightly lower. You will become the owner of the record for the entire next dividend period, making the dividend qualified. You will then receive the next dividend payout AND have to pay lower taxes.

To be honest, there's no true good time or bad time to purchase dividend stocks, in a healthy market. Because of their stable nature, you can really buy them at any time, because the risk of loss can also come at any time. Even if you use the method above, chances are good that things may all become a wash as time goes by. In an unhealthy market, dividend stocks may be the safest choice, but be aware that prices may go up due to good old supply and demand - many investors may be looking for the security of good dividends in an uncertain economy.

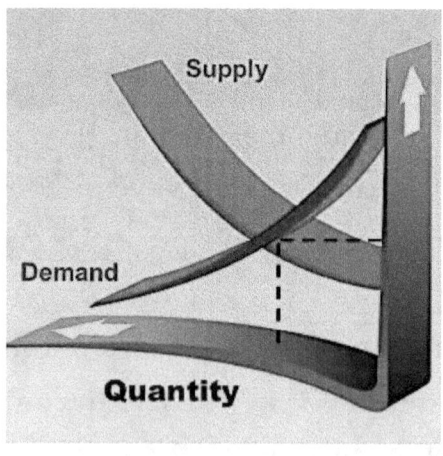

-Price is set at the point where supply meets demand-

It is important to remember that at any given time, each company only has a set number of shares. If those shares are all under ownership, you may have to bid for them or even outbid another investor. This is how the prices of stock get driven up. If no one wants a particular stock, that's when the price falls. The basic principle of supply and demand is what drives the market at any time, no matter how many fancy metrics you learn and read up on.

Doing Splits and Gaining Shares

If a company feels that demand warrants it, they may offer up additional shares of stock or even split their stock, which would immediately increase the number of shares each shareholder owns. This does not have much effect on dividend payouts, because you'll even though the dividend yield has gone down, you'll be receiving the payout on an increased number of stocks. This is especially true of a 2-1 split, which is the most common ratio used. If you own 100 shares of a stock that paid a $1.00 dividend per share, you now own 200 shares with a $0.50 dividend per share. Either way, you make $100 in dividends.

Sometimes, companies want to lower the number of tradeable shares available and will execute a reverse stock split. If this happens, you would now own 50 shares instead of 100, but the dividend payout also stays the same because the yield has not changed. Now, you'll make $100 in dividends as a $2.00 payout on 50 shares.

Sometimes, a company will choose to pay its dividends with a stock payout rather than a cash payout, which we'll discuss more later. For now, let's turn our attention to some of the common mistakes that investors make when they are building or managing a portfolio heavy in dividend stocks.

Chapter 5: Investing Pitfalls- The Big Don'ts and How to Avoid Them

True or false? Everyone makes mistakes. The answer is obviously 'true'. No one is perfect, but when it comes to investing, you don't want to make too many mistakes or you'll be out of money, out of luck, and out of the game. There are several common errors that new investors can fall prey to, so let's go over some of them and talk about how to avoid them.

Don't Cheap Out

One of the most common mistakes that new investors can make is not being able to recognize the difference between low prices and good value. A cheap investment doesn't necessarily equal a good investment, so do your research. You want to make sure you are following your investment plan and try not to speculate on stocks that have a low price tag simply because they are inexpensive.

It may be very tempting to purchase these stocks, but try not to give in unless they truly fit in with your investment goals. It is much better to pass on the temptation than to buy the stock only to find the reason it was so cheap is that the company is tanking. There is a vast difference between price and value, and learning how to distinguish between the two is something that will come with time and experience.

If you're unsure about the prices of any stocks, don't be afraid to seek advice. You may find free advice that will save you money by not buying a stock that's about to plummet, or you may find paid advice that will help you make a profit, but either way, you'll have more money in your pocket than you would if you had invested in a cheap stock that ended up being a bad call.

Don't Believe Everything You Hear

The technology of today means that there's a lot of great advice on investing available at your fingertips. That also means there's a lot of BAD advice on investing floating around out there, too. You can't believe everything you hear, read, or see. It's easy to jump on a stock because a popular host or pundit said that it was a great investment, but you have to remember that those people make their living on being sensational and offering exciting content.

That's not to say that TV analysts or YouTube hosts are wrong, but you'll need to follow up with your own research. Try to not purchase any stocks without examining at least two to three sources. Try to make those sources as current as possible. The internet and daily publications are terrific places to find up to date information, and if you choose to use a broker, they can offer you insight on prices and trends. Magazines are good sources for general advice, but be wary of specific stocks recommended in them. Periodicals are often laid out weeks in advance of publication, and the stock market can change rapidly in that time frame.

You should use common sense when you hear a hot tip. If you are investing in dividend stocks for the long-term, todays hot tip might be tomorrow's big loss. Do some research, and find out why the stock is so 'hot', talk to your broker, and try not to get caught up in the hype. The best investors are the ones who can balance pragmatism and instinct.

Don't Get Caught Up in Yields

Dividend investing is about earning the highest yields, right? So, why wouldn't you want to find all the highest-yield stocks and just snap them up? Because you need to understand why the yields are high so you can make an informed decision on whether or not to make a purchase.

As we briefly touched on earlier, there can be several reasons why a dividend yield is high, and you want to make sure you're purchasing the dividend stock for the correct reason. A high yield can be an indicator of both health and distress in a company, so it is vital to look into why the yield is high. Could the high yield be a 'false positive' of sorts, hiding the fact that the ratio is skewed because stock prices are actually falling?

On the flip side, perhaps a low dividend yield is because a company is slowly and steadily investing money back into new products and new services. In that case, the company may decide to keep yields at a lower percentage while they build equity within. Look to see if the company is showing steadily increasing profits, share prices, and dividend payouts. If they are, it is a good indicator that the stock is worth considering for long-term investment.

Some types of dividends have naturally high yields due to the nature of the companies offering them. Real Estate Investment Trusts or *REITs* are exactly what they sound like; these are companies that allow investors to put their money into a trust which then buys and sells real estate investments. The investor then receives dividends in return.

These investment funds can be an attractive opportunity because they are required to pay out a minimum of 90 percent of their income in dividends to avoid being taxed at standard corporate levels. There are other requirements for REITs which can make them a strong option for dividend investing; they must offer their shares to at least 100 separate stockholders, there cannot be five or fewer holders of more than 50 percent of the shares, the company's income must be at least 75 percent made up of real estate revenue, and at least 75 percent of investment money must go to purchasing real estate assets.

The concept behind a REIT is fairly straightforward. You invest your money into the company, which then buys and sells the property and creates rental opportunities. The capital gains from real estate sales and the rental income are returned to the investors in the form of dividends. When property values go up, rents and gains go up, and dividend payouts go up. REIT income is taxed at the same rate as other dividend income, at either regular or qualified rates, depending on when you became the owner of a record.

Master Limited Partnerships are another investment opportunity for those looking to earn an income on dividends. The structure of an MLP can be a little confusing, but let's break it down:

MLPs are made up of two groups of investors, the general partners, and the limited partners. General partners are the people who are deeply invested in the company, are responsible for the everyday operations, and whose shares in the partnership are not publicly traded. If you wish to invest in an MLP, you'd likely be buying in as a limited partner.

Limited partners in MLPs are there solely to provide a flow of capital into the partnership. They do not have an active role in the company's activities or have decision-making capabilities. However, MLPs, like REITs, are required to pay out at least 90 percent of their investment income as dividends. MLPs are restricted to certain industries, such as commodities, natural resources and energy, and real estate, which means they are relatively stable and have slow growth.

The confusion when investing in MLP's can stem from the tax structure. MLPs do not have to pay corporate taxes, which means that every shareholder, or unitholder (because investors purchase a unit of stocks from the company) must pay their own taxes on their share. If you are using your MLP dividends to fund a retirement account, the tax implications can become even more convoluted. It is highly recommended to use a skilled tax accountant if you become involved in buying MLP shares. However, the return on investment can outweigh the complication of taxes; it is just important to consider all angles before investing in these companies.

Don't Put Blinders On

When you are choosing stocks to invest in, don't fall victim to being closeminded. You may have your heart set on a certain stock or sector, but don't let that blind you to good opportunities elsewhere. It's easy to see established blue chip stocks and go no further, but you may be closing yourself off to smaller, newer companies with amazing potential.

On the flip side, try not to become so enamored with a particular stock that you fail to recognize that they may be a bad investment. You could be setting yourself up for unnecessary financial losses because you were trading with your heart and not your head. It is important to remember that every move you make can affect your bottom line. Remember that every stock you purchase is a tiny bit of ownership in that business, so choose stocks of companies you'd be proud to own!

Don't Ignore the Foreign Markets

American companies are not the only ones who pay out dividend shares, and there are plenty of opportunities to be found in the foreign markets, but you need to know where to look. If you're interested in investing in companies overseas but you're not sure where to get started, don't hesitate to find a global broker who can answer your questions. You can also do extensive online research into foreign markets. The most important thing to learn is how to read the stock charts and currency conversion rates.

By adding foreign stocks to your dividend portfolio, you'll be adding an extra layer of diversity and giving yourself an opportunity to learn about the global economy and how all the markets are interconnected. Foreign investment opportunities can also give you information about the mood of the market in other countries before the markets open in the United States.

One word of mild warning about foreign trading and that word is taxes. When you invest in foreign markets, it is crucial to know what the tax implications could be before you spend your money. Dividend income could be taxed in the country of origin, your country of residence, or both. Make sure the tax rates don't counter any potential income. Much more on taxes will be coming up in the last chapter.

Don't Be Impatient

Dividend stocks are, by their very nature, a slow but steady way to make investment income. If you take your time and find stocks that fit your needs and goals, you will begin seeing a return on your investment with each dividend payout, but it pays to have patience. Because dividend trading is meant to help you build a solid income for the long-term, you can't get frustrated when you don't see large returns right away. In later chapters, we'll talk about ways you can compound your earnings to see larger growth potential.

But if you begin to trade just for the sake of trading, you'll be subject to an excess of transaction fees, not to mention you may miss opportunities for growth if you sell off stock too soon. You should try to limit your larger purchases to one or two a quarter until you've truly got a firm grasp on dividend investing. The point of investing in dividends is to build a stable base for the rest of your portfolio, so make sure you are using your dividend money wisely. You can save the speculation for growth stocks.

Don't Assume Any Investment is 'Safe'

While dividend stocks are so attractive because of their stability, you always need to remain vigilant because there's no such thing as a truly safe investment in the stock market. Like we said earlier, if you think that something seems too good to be true, it probably is.

Companies that are paying dividends at what seems like an abnormally high rate may not be the best investment, because they may not be able to sustain that level of payout. If the market drops suddenly in that company's sector, how would they be able to continue paying high dividend yields, given the price of their stock has probably fallen? These are things you'll need to consider when you are choosing stocks for your portfolio.

It is easy to say that your dividend stocks are 'safe' because of their stable nature, but the stock market can be a volatile place, so it is as important to watch your dividend stocks as closely as you would any other investment. With a little diligence and a lot of common sense, you can make sure that your dividend stocks are as safe as stocks probably can be.

Now that we've gone over the key points of research and talked about how to avoid common pitfalls, let's talk about the market itself. How can you learn to read the market, recognize trends, and know-how and when to cut your losses? In the next chapter, we'll examine how to become adept at being a savvy stock evaluator.

Chapter 6: Reading the Market

The stock market, as you've no doubt come to realize, has its own language and its own personality. Stocks can be an indicator of the health of an economy and consumer confidence. We also know that studying the history of the stock market can make you a better student of the stock market in the present. How can you learn to recognize trends and truly read the market? It takes a bit of study, but once you discover what to look for and where to find the data, you'll be able to see patterns and analyze news that will help you determine the mood of the market and where it's headed next.

Take Lessons from History

The stock market is not a new institution, and there are important lessons to be learned from the past. The Great Depression, recessions, inflation, and the more recent bursting of the mortgage bubble and so-called Great Recession are just a few of the economic downturns throughout history that were either caused by issues within the stock market or had a negative impact on the market in their aftermath.

They say that those who don't know history are doomed to repeat it, and the American economy has taken some heavy hits in its short time as a free, industrialized nation. Before we delve into today and tomorrow's market, let's go into a couple of the events that define the lowest points in the United States' financial history. By first looking at the Great Depression of the early 20th century and the Great Recession of the early 21st century, we can begin to define patterns that contributed to both economic crises, and why they share so many similarities, but are also very different events.

First, we'll examine the Great Depression, which was the worst and longest economic disaster to affect the modernized world. Several factors contributed to the Great Depression, not the least of which was the stock market crash of 1929. What led to the market plummeting and what were the long-term impacts?

During the 1920s, America experienced a period of rapid economic growth and social change that was dubbed the Roarin' Twenties. During this decade, consumer confidence was high, and employment was relatively easy to find and maintain as factories popped up and industry boomed in the wake of the end of the First World War. Everyone had faith in the stock market, and shares were bought by everyone from business tycoons to low-income workers. People poured their life savings into the market, and many bought stock 'on margin'- meaning with borrowed money.

In August of 1929, the stock market was at an all-time high, but a spending slowdown signaled a change in the balance of supply and demand. Products went unsold, and so, fewer capital dollars went into production and manufacturing. At the same time, the Midwest, America's breadbasket, was experiencing a drought of epic proportions, which was hindering the growth of commodity crops like wheat and corn. Things came to a head in October of 1929, when the bottom dropped out of the stock market.

With crops failing, factories slowing, and unemployment on the rise, the stock market took its first major hit on October 24, 1929, when nervous investors began a mass sell which would cause the market to exchange a record 12 million shares that day. That record would be broken just days later, on October 29, when 16 million shares were sold. That day is now known as Black Tuesday, and it left many investors destitute, holding worthless stocks. Those who had purchased their shares on margin were now left with crippling debt.

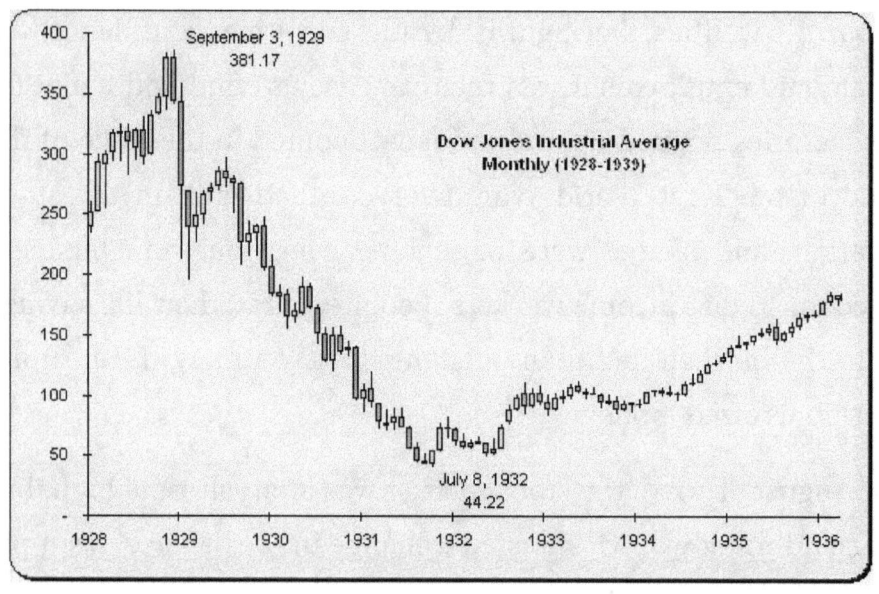

- The market crash of October 1929 took several years to recover from-

What followed the stock market crash was a series of events that turned what could have been a recoverable event into a major economic crisis. With consumer confidence at an all-time low and unemployment at an all-time high - nearly 6 million Americans were out of work by 1931 - factories closed and farms were abandoned. People felt that they could no longer trust any financial institutions, and the crisis was worsened by a rash of bank runs.

Bank runs occur when a bank's customers decide that they want to pull their money out of their accounts, but the bank doesn't have enough cash on hand to satisfy the customers' demands. Most banks don't actually store a person's savings in a vault - when you deposit money with a bank, the bank uses that money for other things, with the knowledge that it will be available to you when you choose to retrieve it. If you'd like a large sum of your money, it is now customary to go to the bank for a cashier's check or arrange with your branch to make a large cash withdrawal. Most, if not all, modern banks and credit unions are protected by the FDIC or Federal Deposit Insurance Corporation.

The FDIC wasn't created until 1933 when the Banking Act was passed by the United States Congress. Prior to that, money was not insured when it was deposited into a bank, which is why the bank runs of 1930-1933 were so devastating to the banks themselves. Several thousand banks went defunct after the bank runs, unable to pay their customers their funds.

With the drought in the Midwest, farmers packed up their families and their meager belongings and migrated to cities looking for work, most famously chronicled in John Steinbeck's seminal 1939 novel *The Grapes of Wrath*. When the farmers reached their destinations, however, they found work to be scarce and conditions along the road and eventually in government-run resettlement camps to be inhumane and unlivable.

The Great Depression led to global economic repercussions due to the world's reliance on the gold standard, a monetary system by which the value of all currencies is linked directly to the price of gold. The United States used the gold standard prior to and during the Great Depression, but no longer follows the system primarily due to its inability to maintain the standard during the depression era. Because of this, and because of a lack of goods to export, the global economy took a hit from the crisis in America.

The Great Depression took a turn with the election of Franklin D. Roosevelt in 1932. By the time Roosevelt was inaugurated in March of 1933, nearly 15 million Americans were unemployed, and about one-third of American banks had been shuttered. Roosevelt, a Democrat, replaced the Republican Herbert Hoover who had not done much to aid in the crisis. Hoover believed that it was a problem of the people and not of the government. Roosevelt took a much different stance on the crisis and began almost immediately to implement his New Deal economic recovery initiative.

Within his first few months in office, Roosevelt ordered all banks shut down while Congress passed industry-saving legislation, including the creation of the FDIC and the Securities and Exchange Commission (SEC), which regulates the stock market. He created jobs through programs like the TVA and WPA, and also created Social Security to assure that all Americans would have income guaranteed after retirement.

The United States was well on the road to economic recovery by the late 1930s, with slow but sure progress to lessen unemployment and restore America's farmlands. The advent of World War II also helped the American and global economy because wartime meant an increased need for armament and aircraft production. The depression was officially declared over by the time the United States entered the conflict after the bombing of Pearl Harbor in December of 1941.

The Great Depression was a confluence of several unfortunate economic events, but there are lessons to be taken away from the crisis. First, no single part of the economy stands alone; agriculture, industry, and all other sectors depend on the health of each other. Second, lack of governmental oversight led to unregulated and wildly speculative stock trading, implausible mortgages and loans, and undue amounts of credit being given. The creation of the FDIC and SEC prevent the market and the banking industry from getting that out of control again.

The biggest lesson to be learned from the Great Depression, however, is that there are always signs of the health of the economy. There were people who predicted the stock market crash, but they were in the minority, and most others wanted to believe that the American economic boom of the 20s was too big to fail, a phrase used in more recent times to describe some of the big banks and finance houses that fell during the Great Recession in 2008-09. The Great Depression should be used as a teaching tool for how not to ignore the signals that the stock market and the economy are sending out.

While the Great Depression was obviously a massive economic crisis, all the signs were there that should have caused more concern than people showed. Because of these lessons, the Great Recession of 2008-2009 could have been a lot worse than it was. The Great Recession was caused by a number of factors both similar and differing from the cause of the Great Depression and affected real estates, banking, and markets worldwide.

At the root of the Great Recession which, by the International Monetary Fund's definition based on the gross domestic product, technically began in the United States in December of 2007, is what's known as the subprime mortgage crisis. Subprime mortgages are those that are given to those with historically bad credit, making them high-interest and high-risk loans.

Because many of these loans were at risk of never being paid back, the loans started to be sold in bulk by the originators to larger financial institutions, which we're hoping to make a quick profit from the default of the loans. While the housing market was still healthy, some of the loan originators began to lose solvency, and when mortgage giant Freddy Mac announced in early 2007 that they would no longer be buying up subprime mortgages, the smaller loan originators began going out of business.

Other large institutions followed suit, leaving millions of homeowners with mortgages that were worth more than the cost of their homes, and leaving the mortgage owners with millions of worthless loans. At the same time, the stock market was reaching a record peak, trading at an unheard of 14,000 shares on a single day in October 2007. This record high was followed by an 18-month drop by nearly half that trading volume, falling to 6,500 shares traded. Investors saw the loss of their life savings, and the net worth of American households fell by $14 trillion, yes, trillion dollars from 2007 to 2009.

With the economy on the brink of collapsing, the Fed took the unprecedented action of reducing the nation's target interest rate to zero percent. The hope was that it would encourage anyone with money left to invest to stimulate the economy, but that alone wasn't enough. Then-president George W. Bush signed a stimulus package that gave taxpayer rebates, reduced tax rates, and introduced higher limits on mortgage loans to urge people to purchase homes and revive the housing market.

Despite the boost from the government, financial giants continued to collapse under the weight of too many subprime mortgages. Lehman Brothers filed the largest corporate bankruptcy in American history, and Bear Stearns was forced out of business and quickly sold off all its remaining assets to JP Morgan Chase at a fraction of their original worth. The government then swooped in and rescued investing firm AIG before they too could fail, giving them a loan of some $85 billion to stay solvent. The government held that if AIG also collapsed, the American economy would be destroyed.

Having staved off the failure of AIG, the government turned its attention to bailing out other struggling corporations by passing the TARP (Troubled Asset Relief Program) in October of 2008. This program gave the government nearly $700 billion in relief funding to loan to businesses and corporations to inject capital and keep them afloat until the market could correct itself. Using some of the funds, the government bought the assets of several large banks and then used some of the funding to bail out General Motors, Bank of America, and the Chrysler Corporation.

In January 2009, Barack Obama replaced George W. Bush as president (The Republican Herbert Hoover was ousted for the Democrat Franklin D. Roosevelt, so doesn't that sound a little familiar?). Obama brought with him new economic policies but also inherited the recession. Obama was quick to institute new tax breaks and authorize spending on infrastructure and education, as well as green energy and health care. By June of 2009, unemployment was down, earnings were on the upswing, and the Great Recession was declared officially over in the United States.

The global downturn wasn't yet over in Europe, however, where several countries were forced to take loans from the European Union to stay afloat amongst the financial crisis. Having defaulted on their debts, countries like Greece, Ireland, and Portugal among others, were forced into austerity budgets to try to right their sinking economic ships.

If you'll recall, one of the outcomes of the Great Depression was the signing of the Banking Act of 1933. An integral part of that legislation was the Glass-Steagall Act, which regulated a separation between commercial banks and investment banks. In the 1970s, large commercial banks began to argue that being separated from being able to invest was impeding their business, and by 1987, the Fed's then-chairman Alan Greenspan all but encouraged those banks to find loopholes to begin investing as 'affiliates'.

The issue came to head when the Glass-Steagall Act was effectively repealed in 1999 by legislation signed by President Bill Clinton, known as the Financial Services Modernization Act or Gramm-Leach-Bliley Act. Less than a decade after, the Great Recession struck, and while some economists argue that phasing out Glass-Steagall was the largest contributing factor, others disagreed. In 2010, President Obama signed the Dodd-Frank Act, placing some of the previous regulations back upon the banking industry.

In truth, the loss of the government regulations that were granted by the Glass-Steagall Act did play a role in the Great Recession, but so also did poor regulation of the subprime mortgage market, inflated credit scores, and a securities market that spiraled out of control. With Obama's signing of the Dodd-Frank Act, the government will be allowed to seize control of failing banking institutions, and safeguards were put into place to protect consumer investments and discourage predatory lending.

The fact that the government was quick to step in during the Great Recession is one thing that makes it stand apart from the laissez-faire attitude of the government in 1929 and through the election of Roosevelt in 1932. That government awareness and assistance is probably what saved the Great Recession from becoming the Second Great Depression.

Now that we've had a bit of a history lesson, let's go over how to learn to read the market for today and for the future. We'll talk about how to analyze the data for individual stocks first, then move on to how to study sectors and overall markets. By the end of this chapter, you'll be able to recognize trends within a stock on its own, within a sector as a whole, and as they relate to the entirety of the market.

Reading the Signs

When you look at a stock chart for the first time, it can be a confusing mass of numbers, abbreviations, symbols, and lines. What you really want to look at is the *trend line,* which is the line that denotes the price of a stock over time. With the rise of the internet, it is easy to find stock charts that have interactive interfaces on which you can adjust the time frame to see how a stock has historically performed.

The trend line is vastly important to how we consider stocks for purchase. It gives vital insights into how a stock routinely performs, when it has dipped and climbed, and how the price has fluctuated. When you look at a stock's price over the course of several years, and you see a large drop or large increase, it gives you a clue that something significant probably happened during that time frame. You can search for news about the company during that time frame to discover the cause of the drastic price change.

When a company's stock rapidly goes up in price, it is often due to the announcement of a new product or service; usually, something that's been highly anticipated like a new technological device or a new pharmaceutical treatment. When a company's stock drops rapidly, it could be caused by a change of leadership, like the drop in Apple stock when Steve Jobs retired in 2011, or by catastrophic product failure or a scandalous event. In recent news, aeronautics giant Boeing experienced a stock drop after the crash of two of its 737 Max jets, causing numerous fatalities.

The point is, reading the trend line by itself isn't enough. When you see the trend line change quickly in one direction or the other, you should investigate why. Once you've done a little research into what caused drastic price changes for a company's stock in the past, you should next research what the company is planning to do in the near future and in the long-term. Some of this information should be in the company's annual report or can be found by looking at industry websites and journals. If you know that a company's stock has historically risen when they've released a certain type of product, and they are planning on releasing the newest version of that product soon, it pays to know when that product will be available so that you can purchase shares ahead of the release.

Reading the trends for one business need not be tricky, and once you've got that skill under your belt, you can look into the larger trends of an industry or sector. Many times, competitors within a sector will release similar new products within a very small time frame, like new video game consoles or other technologies. Other sectors ramp up the release of new products and services before the winter holiday shopping season, and so it's worth looking into what's ahead for those sectors.

The industrial sector is often dependent on the prices of raw materials, so if you're investigating stocks in that sector, you should make a note to read up on what's happening with the trade of raw materials, which can be affected by supply and demand as well as fluctuations in tariffs. The real estate sector is affected by interest rates, so you can take the time to look at the current rates and find out if the Fed will be raising or lowering rates soon.

The point is, common sense comes into play when you are investigating trends within a sector. Sector swings can be determined by the time of year, global supply and demand, and industry regulation. If you are looking into purchasing shares in more than one company from a particular sector, you need to look at the sector as a whole before investing. Be sure to examine if any new laws will be coming into play that may affect certain industries or sectors. This could be manufacturing regulations, restrictions or allowances on food, drink, or pharmaceuticals, or a change in tax structures.

Learning to read trends in the overall market is your next step. The stock market is the main indicator of global economic health, and it rises and falls as other factors rise and fall. As you've no doubt seen by now, consumer confidence and unemployment are two of these factors. Other things that affect how the stock market moves are interest rates, political climate, and supply and demand. There's also the bandwagon effect (a major cause of the crash of 1929) and inflation.

Consumer confidence plays a huge role in how the market moves. The consumer confidence index is a measure of how optimistic or pessimistic people are about the economy. A higher consumer confidence index means that people believe the economy is steady or on the upswing and they are more willing to invest their money into that economy. A lower index shows that people are less will to spend and more likely to save, fearing the proverbial rainy day. Unemployment ties heavily into consumer confidence because higher unemployment rates mean that people have less money to contribute to the economy.

When people have less to spend, it affects supply and demand. Remember the consumer slowdown right before the stock market crashed in 1929? People spent less money, causing supply to go up and demand to go down. With demand down, factories slowed or halted production. With a decrease in production, there was a need for fewer workers. That led to higher unemployment. Surely, you can see how this vicious circle led to an economy that spiraled out of control, leading to the Great Depression.

Consumer confidence and unemployment are measurable statistics that you can observe when you do your research. Supply and demand are not as easily measured, but almost always follows suit of the other two indicators. If you can see a distinct downturn, you may want to adjust your investment strategies accordingly.

The government also has a lot to do with how the stock market behaves. The interest rates set by the Fed can send the stock market into a frenzy with high volumes of shares being traded ahead of anticipated rate changes. Be vigilant about this, especially when you are focusing on dividend stocks. Because dividend stocks are relatively stable, you don't have to worry too much about price changes with a change in the federal interest rate, but you may see your dividends grow or shrink when the rate is adjusted.

The political climate can also have a strong effect on the economy. If we refer back to our history of the Great Depression, we can see that the uncapped boom that eventually led to the crash was in the wake of the end of World War I. People were glad to be done with war, they were starting businesses and families, buying houses and cars and stocks without a care. It was too good to be true, and when the bubble burst, everything came crashing down.

The Great Depression only began to turn around with a change in leadership, as Americans fed up with the crisis elected Franklin D. Roosevelt to replace Herbert Hoover. Hoover had taken a hands-off approach to the financial crisis, whereas Roosevelt promised to do something about it - a promise which he kept by beginning the public works projects that began to employ millions. He also introduced regulatory practices that are still in effect today and implemented Social Security. While all this helped tremendously, remember that it was the beginning of World War II which truly healed the American economy.

If you take a look at historical stock data, you'll notice that there are almost always swings right around the times of major political events, such as presidential elections. Investors are often holding their breath or biding their time to see what the outcome of a major election will be, not wanting to inject too much capital into a market that may be affected by a new president's economic policies. Policies like sanctions and tariffs can affect foreign trade and domestic production.

Inflation is also controlled by the government. In the United States, this is under the purview of the Central Bank. Inflation sounds complicated, but let's simplify it. At its most basic, inflation is a measure of buying power. It is the increase in the price of goods/services and the decrease in the purchasing power of the currency. Inflation can best be described by an older person telling a teenager, "When I was your age, it only cost $2 to go the movies!"

What that older person is describing is inflation. A dollar is not worth now what it was worth ten, twenty, fifty, a hundred years ago. Its buying power has steadily decreased over time, causing it to be worth less. Why is buying power such a crucial number? In the real world, buying power is a measure of how much of a product or service you can get for a dollar.

In 1950, that would have meant a loaf of bread and a gallon of milk. In 2019, that dollar might get you a slice of bread and a cup of milk. Maybe. The buying power of your dollar went down over time because the cost of goods and services went up. The

Central Bank attempts to control inflation by monitoring interest rates and economic growth. It is possible to invest your money to beat inflation, but you need to be savvy about it.

In the market, buying power refers to the amount of money an investor has free to invest. This total includes the balance of your brokerage account, plus any other investment money that could be taken on margin. In short, your buying power in the stock market is the total of every available dollar that you have that could be reinvested back into the market. This is important because the buying power of your dollar bill at the corner store and the buying power of your $10,000 brokerage account are subject to the same rate of inflation, and suffer the same consequences when inflation gets too high.

This is why so many investors like dividend stocks when inflation is on the rise. Dividend stocks are a stable way to get your money into the market before the value of the dollar decreases again. While the old saying says that a penny saved is a penny earned, you need to remember that if you don't invest your money, it will have no opportunity to grow at all. Cash under a mattress will ALWAYS depreciate over time due to inflation, but the money that's invested will have a chance at beating the system.

None of these factors exist in a vacuum, so it's important to look at the economy as a living entity that relies on the health of each factor to function properly. When you are deciding how and where to spend your investment funds, it is crucial to understand the state of the economy as a whole. Look for the sectors that are performing well, and study their historical data and their upcoming offerings. You want to make sure you have the whole picture before making any decisions. Studying the past performance and future projections for each stock and sector you want to invest in will give you all the information you'll need to invest wisely.

When you've effectively become a student of the economy, you'll be able to identify trends that will help you to be a savvier investor. While there is always a risk when you put your money into the stock market, fervently reading and analyzing data will work towards mitigating that risk. The more informed you are, the better you will strategize your investing.

In the next chapter, we'll look at how to handle your dividend investments to include high-yield stocks. While the lure of high dividends can be appealing, high-yield dividends come with their own set of risks. Let's look at how you can add these stocks to your portfolio without breaking the bank or risking too much.

Chapter 7: High Yields and How to Handle Them

Earlier in this book, we briefly touched upon high-yield dividends and what that yield can mean for your portfolio. In this chapter, we'll take an in-depth look at the risks and rewards of high-yield dividends and how you be confident in purchasing high-yield dividends that fit your investment goals. High-yield dividends can be a valuable part of any portfolio, but as with any dividend stock, your research will be the key to your success.

Remember to ask "Why?"

Nothing is more attractive to an investor than a stock with high-yield dividends or a high return on investment. It is easy to see the yield and want to jump on that stock. Take a deep breath, and remember to ask yourself, "Why?" Why is the dividend yield so high? What other economic factors could be behind the high yield, and is the yield going to be sustainable?

These are important questions that need to be answered before investing in a high-yield dividend. Sustainability is a key factor because a company can decide to lower or cease dividends at any time. Is it a new company trying to attract investors? It may be that they are being unreasonably optimistic about their earnings potential and won't be able to maintain that level of payout. While you, as an investor, might like to get in on the ground floor of new stock, it might also be prudent to observe this one for a while before investing.

Another key piece of data to look at is the current interest rate. Could the interest rate be driving the yield ratio? In some sectors, like banking, the interest rate plays heavily into the price of their stock. When interest rates go down, stock prices go up. The reverse is also true. While banking stocks tend to have high dividend yield, remember that the dividend yield is dependent on the value of the stock itself.

Sometimes, yields seem high because a stock price is inflated. Be sure to look at the stock's trends over time to see if they seem overvalued. A bad economy can force some companies into paying dividends beyond their means just to appease their stockholders. This is not a sound strategy for the company, and it would not be a sound strategy for you to invest in them. You'll probably want to avoid stocks that show these characteristics, despite the siren's song of high dividends.

Dividend investing is meant to be a slow, steady way to increase your stock income, so when choosing high-yield dividends, do all your research before investing. Things that seem too good to be true often are. Companies that are paying out high yields are not using that capital to reinvest in their business, so be sure to examine what the company's future plans hold. This information should be found in their annual report literature or on their website under 'news' or 'press releases'. You want to soak up as much data as you can before purchasing a high-yield dividend.

Taking the Plunge into High Yields

Once you've done your research and decided that you'd like to try adding some high-yield dividends to your portfolio, you can use all the data you've collected to decide which ones to purchase. Typically, you will see the most high-yield stocks in the utilities, communications, and consumer goods sectors, but don't discount the role that technology stocks play in an ever-evolving market. While tech stocks have historically chosen to reinvest capital into research and development, in recent years, more tech companies have begun to offer dividends and at a fairly high yield.

While you need to have patience when it comes to building dividend income, you can look at stocks in the tech sector as being on the edge of traditional and high-yield, because of the maturation of the industry over the last few decades. Perhaps, it is because as consumers, we have come to expect so much of the tech sector we aren't really blown away by every 'next big thing' anymore. We've begun to be a little jaded, and technology, especially new devices, seems to have lost a little of its 'wow' factor.

The recent trend in high-yield dividends in the tech sector may also be because the leaders in the technology industry are now the second, and sometimes, third generation to be developing these shiny new things, and have learned business savvy along the way. While the technology used to be the purview of outliers, it has become so mainstream, and many of the industry leaders have become mainstream, as well. Whatever the reason, tech stocks are becoming very attractive dividend options these days.

Don't Disregard the Classics

While it can be very tempting to buy into stocks that seem very exciting, don't forget that companies that have been in existence for decades, even centuries, have lasted so long for a reason. Many corporations in the communications industry have been around since the advent of the business, and still, continue to pay out dividends at a level higher than the average.

Think about your favorite local business. Why are they so highly regarded? Perhaps, it's a family-owned business that's been passed through several generations. Maybe they offer their customers perks such as a savings card or loyalty rewards. Those are the businesses that we all like to frequent and that we recommend to others.

It is by that analogy that you should look at dividend stocks. A company that has operated continuously with happy customers for many years is often one that will have the most stable dividends with above-average dividends. Research the companies in each sector that are the oldest and most established, and you'll be sure to find one or two in every industry that can offer you the types of dividends you're looking for.

Be Wary of Traps

There's a term surrounding high-yield dividends known as the *dividend trap*. What this means is that a company draws in new investors by offering a high dividend yield, but the company is not stable enough to continue to pay that dividend over time. In short, it is a bad buy. This is like a gym that offers a low rate for new members, but then charges a lot of money once your initiation period is over. It seems like such a bargain at the time, but now you're trapped in a situation where you're being overcharged and underserved. You want to get out, but you're worried that you've already wasted so much money, you keep going to the gym and praying you can find an exit strategy for your membership. You don't want to feel the same way about your stocks, so how can you avoid a dividend trap?

If you've done your research, you'll know not to take a high-yield dividend at face value. If something strikes you as off with a company's dividend payout, look at the rest of the sector. A company offering a much higher dividend yield than its competitors and peers should be a red flag to you. Take the time to closely examine why the company is able to pay out at a higher rate than others like it.

Knowing the difference between a price trend and a price shock is also helpful. Because of the way dividend yield is calculated, we know that a price drop can artificially make the yield higher. When a price drops, is it consistently dropping in a trend? If so, it is probably best to avoid buying that stock- the loss of money on the stock will not likely be offset by any dividend payout.

If the stock seems to have experienced a sharp drop due to an unforeseen circumstance or a bad market week, it may be worth it to snap up some shares before the stock goes back on the upswing. This is one of those judgment calls that requires thought and research, but also requires a bit of instinct. If the stock has historically been a good performer with a high yield, go ahead and buy. But be sure to keep a close eye on the stock and take action if it does not head back on the uptick. The market as a whole can also affect dividend yields, so be vigilant about whether or not the market is on an upswing or a downswing.

The other metric you can check when you're suspicious about a dividend trap is cash flow. When a company is troubled, its cash flow will begin to slow or dry up. Be wary of companies offering high dividend yields while their earnings or cash flow stagnate or decline. Dividends cannot be paid out without the cash to back them, so make sure you don't get caught in a sticky situation with stocks like these.

Options for Using Your High-Yield Income

When you've invested in high-yield dividends, you'll obviously want to do something with the income. Do you want to use it for a large purchase, like a home or car? Are you using it as a rainy day fund or supplementing retirement income? What you want the income for can dictate how you handle your high-yield dividend investments.

Younger people who get involved with dividend investing are often looking for a way to finance a lifestyle. This could include making money to pay for college or pay back existing student loans, buying a home or vehicle, or financing life events like weddings. With a small portfolio of dividend stocks, it's possible to make enough income over a few years to fund these goals and leave the stock market behind forever.

These days, many younger investors are getting into dividend stocks for the long haul, fearful that they may not be able to retire in the same manner that the generations before them did. An economy is an uncertain place for everyone, but for the younger generations who are struggling to find work after college, coupled with student loans and the fear that they'll never find affordable housing, it's a very different economic climate than it was for their parents and grandparents. Dividend investing can offer a sense of financial security no matter what the future holds.

For older investors, the stock market may be a way to fund retirement or set money aside for their children and grandchildren. High-yield dividends are a great way to build a stable, passive income that can be used for everyday living expenses, travel, unforeseen medical expenses, etc. There are ways to set aside your income to prepare for all your goals and any emergency eventualities.

The one part of dividend investing that we haven't touched upon yet is re-investing your income into the market. Many people choose to take their dividend payout and either fold it back into the purchase of stocks in other companies or take their dividend payout in the form of more stock from the company paying the dividend. Some companies even pay their dividends in the form of shares rather than cash (called a *stock dividend*). With a stock dividend, you now own more shares of the company than you did before.

There are some things to be wary about when it comes to stock dividends. One is that a company that is paying out shares rather than cash may have a cash flow issue. You should investigate that possibility and handle it in the manner we've previously discussed. The second is to be aware if the company is offering either stock or cash payout on their dividends. If the answer is yes, shareholders can be paid in either form, you should know that should you choose the stock payout, it will be taxed at the same rate as a cash payout.

Moving Your Dividend Income

One other thing to consider doing with your dividend income is moving it into another account. We've talked about the importance of keeping your market money separate from other funds, and if you are investing to build savings or set aside money for a specific purpose, you might want to transfer your dividend income, especially high-yield income, into a new account, like a retirement fund or high-interest savings account.

By doing this, you can assure yourself that you will not be risking more than you can afford to spend on additional stock while maintaining the dividend income you've done so much research to gain. An IRA, or individual retirement account, can easily be set up with your bank or financial planner. By transferring funds into an IRA, you can begin to set yourself up for a diverse portfolio that includes a stable savings fund which you can borrow from yourself if needed, and the flexibility of your market fund to purchase more stock. Be aware that you will still be taxed on your dividends and your IRA, but the tax rates will vary by bracket.

The exception to this tax is what's known as a Roth IRA, and there are advantages to having your dividend payouts deposited directly into an account of this type. The dividend payouts will not be subject to income tax; however, the downside is that a Roth Ira cannot be used collateral for loans, and income from foreign investments may be taxed at their country of origin. We'll talk more about the Roth IRA when we talk about taxes in Chapter 10.

- You can use your dividend income to save up for retirement-

Another place you might want to move your dividend income is into a high-interest savings account or CD (certificate of deposit). This is another way of assuring yourself that you've got the money you cannot touch. High-interest savings accounts are insured by the FDIC up to $250,000, so this is a fairly safe place to let your money work for you while you focus on other investments. These accounts usually have low fees and low minimum balances. The downside to these types of savings accounts is that they often take a few days to transfer funds and usually only come with online banking capability but without ATM access.

A Certificate of Deposit, or CD, account is another way to set aside some of your dividend earnings where you are unlikely to touch the principle. A CD account is fairly simple and is a wonderful way to save for a one-time event or expense, like a large purchase or a dream vacation. When you put money into a CD, you work with the financial institution to determine how long a CD you'd like; most short-term CDs are for two years, with longer options of 3-5 years or even 10 years available.

Once you've chosen the length of your CD, you should also decide if you want it to have a fixed, variable, or adjustable interest rate. Fixed-rate guarantees that you'll be paid at the same rate no matter what happens with interest rates while the CD is maturing. A variable interest rate moves with adjustments in the rate by the Fed. An adjustable-rate CD allows you to change the interest rate, but only a limited number of times without penalty. You will also incur penalties if you withdraw the money before the maturity date, making CDs an attractive option for those who have a hard time resisting the urge to move money around. No one wants to cause themselves the loss of income.

Money market accounts are another option for those who'd like to move their dividend income into a separate financial space. These types of savings accounts usually have exceptional interest rates, but may require a larger initial deposit to open. They make an excellent source of emergency income because of their liquidity and are insured by the FDIC. They aren't to be confused with money market mutual funds; those investments are NOT insured. A money market account is attractive for its high-interest rates, but be aware that you will be subject to taxes. These accounts are also not ideal for everyday use- they have limited transactions per month. However, if you have the willpower to resist moving money in and out of a money market account, you can easily reap the benefits of the interest.

However, you choose to save or spend your dividend income, it is important to do your research. Talk to your broker, your banker, your financial planner, and your investing friends to get ideas on what works best for saving your high-yield earnings. We'll talk more about spending that money later on, but in the next chapter, we'll go over ways to avoid paying too much for your dividend stocks.

Chapter 8: The Price is Right

No one wants to pay too much for anything, right? The same goes for dividend stocks. You want your goal to be to get as much bang for your buck so you can maximize both your stock earnings and your dividend returns. Let's talk about finding the right time to buy and how you can avoid purchasing stocks at an overvalued price.

Identifying Values

When you are looking at the value of any long-term investment, including dividend stocks, you want to look at several factors. The first is the price. How much something costs is the most crucial piece of knowledge you can have. The second is appreciation or depreciation. This is a measurement of how much value an investment gains or loses over time. Ideally, you want your stocks to be something that adds value, not loses it.

Investments like vehicles tend to depreciate. Real estate values fluctuate with the market. But stock values are the most difficult to pinpoint, and with good reason. Unlike the real estate market, which goes in cycles parallel to the overall economy, stock values change *every single day*. In an earlier chapter, we talked about reading the market and reading individual stocks, so it's time to put that knowledge into play.

When you look at a stock chart, you'll often see a market evaluation letting you know how the analysts feel about the value of a stock. While you are free to take their advice at face value, you can also do your own due diligence in determining if a stock is a good buy.

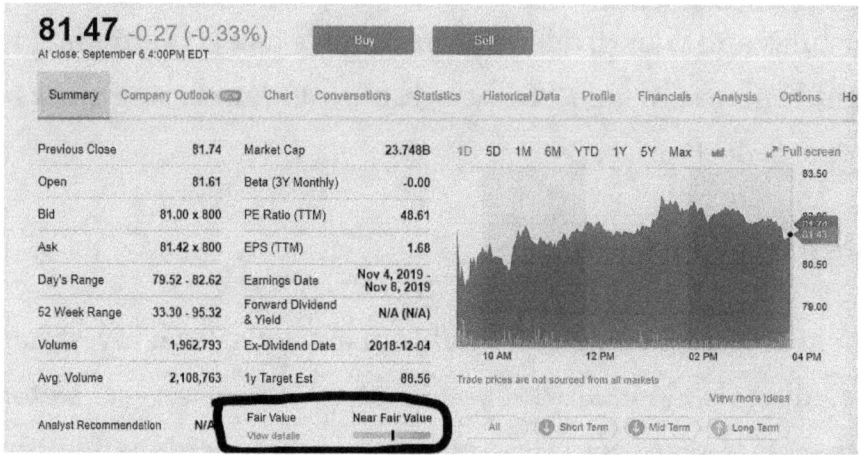

- Most market reports will show you a stock valuation for market value-

You want to look at many of the things we talked about when we discussed reading the market, but in this case, you're going to focus on the individual stock. How has the value trended over time, including the dividend yield and the dividend per share? Does the stock value seem in line with the values throughout its sector and industry?

While it is true that there are times that you need to trade on gut instinct, dividend stocks are not meant to be bought and sold quickly. There is a practice known as *dividend capture*, which most brokers and financial planners will advise you to stay away from. Dividend capture involves purchasing a dividend stock right before the dividend is paid out, usually on the last day to become the owner of a record, and then selling the stock as soon as the dividend is paid. It's not a sound strategy for purchasing stocks at their proper value, nor is it a sound strategy for ensuring solid dividend income.

Let's get back to making proper stock valuations so that you can choose stocks that fit your lifestyle, your budget, and your goals. We know that stock prices for dividend stocks often fall right after the dividend pays out, so you can use that as a starting point to decide if the price is low enough to buy or if you'd like to wait. You don't want to wait too long, because you can predict that the stock price will rise again heading towards the next dividend payout.

Setting aside the old standards, how do you evaluate a bargain buy in new companies that lack a long track record? You can look at their daily reports and read up on their annual reports and investor literature. You're looking for the release of the company's next product or new service, and you'll want to purchase your shares before that release date if you feel that the company truly will be offering the next big thing. Don't wait too long, or you'll run the risk of being priced out once the product hits.

Bargain Hunting

When you are looking for a low-cost, long-term value investment dividend stocks can be found by looking at a few key metrics, the first being the P/E ratio, which we discussed earlier. The P/E, or price to earnings ratio can be a crucial indicator of the value of a stock. The next metric you want to look at is the growth rate. By using these two indicators together, you can calculate the PEG ratio or price/earnings to growth. PEG ratio is determined by dividing the P/E ratio by the growth rate.

You can use the PEG ratio to decide if a stock is overvalued, fairly valued, or undervalued. A fairly priced stock is considered to have a PEG ratio of 1, meaning that the P/E ratio and the growth rate are equal. Anything higher than 1 indicates that a stock is overvalued, and anything less means the stock is undervalued. Using this knowledge, you can choose stocks that have great potential for earnings and for providing adequate to substantial dividends.

When you see a stock that is undervalued, you should do just a little more research before you buy it. Make sure you know the reason or reasons why the stock is priced so low, to make sure there is no fundamental problem with the company. Ask yourself:

- Is the price low because of something affecting the entire industry or sector?

- Is the price low because the company isn't very exciting?

- Is the price low because the market is on an overall downswing?

- Is the price low because there is something wrong with the company itself?

- Is the price low because of a recent stock split?

- Is the price low because of a recent reverse stock split?

Once you've discovered the answer, you can make a final determination on whether or not a bargain stock is worth purchasing. Be sure that when you do your research, you that seems like an amazing deal, only to find out that the company was cheap and paying out high-yield dividends as a last gasp effort to inject cash and avoid insolvency. Be sure you are still checking all your key metrics before jumping on the bargain train. Just because something is the cheapest option, doesn't mean it is the best option.

Expect the Best, Prepare for the Worst

When you buy anything at a bargain, you often find that you get what you pay for. If you buy a cheap pair of shoes, nine times out of ten, they will fall apart more quickly than a more expensive pair of shoes. That tenth time, you will get a bargain that is also a value- a pair of shoes that don't fall apart in weeks.

The same goes for bargain stocks. You want to find that one-in-ten pair of shoes, but you may feel like you find more lemons than you do gems. You need to be prepared for the possibility that the bargain stock you bought may not have been such a steal. That's one of the reasons we keep our market money separate from our other finances. You need to make sure your market money can take the hit of buying a subpar stock, and it will happen. Everyone from the greenest trader to the most experienced broker on Wall Street has bought a bum stock from time to time.

If and when you do see the bottom fall out on a stock you had high hopes for, don't despair. That's why you keep a cushion in your brokerage account; to make up for any negative impact from a bad choice. This is not to say you should ever buy stocks that you have a bad feeling about just because you have the cushion there. You always want to expect the best, but just be prepared for the worst. That's why market research is the best practice any trader can employ. Numbers don't lie. That's one of the beautiful things about the stock market; there are hundreds of statistics you can look at to paint a complete picture, but math is always honest.

Bargain hunting for stocks is not the easiest task. You'll want to make a list of stocks you are interested in and run the numbers for each. You should start with at least 20 to 25 stocks and begin to narrow your list based on your research and number crunching. Try to narrow your list down to ten stocks. Those are the ones you should begin observing to see how they perform daily for a few days or a week. Once you've done some thorough observation, you can choose which of those ten to purchase, if not all of them. Then start the process all over again.

One tool that's very useful for searching for bargain stocks is an online system known as a stock screener. It is exactly what it sounds like and it can help you sort through stocks based on price and any other number of criteria. It is not particularly recommended for in-depth research on high-cost shares, but it is a very good place to find bargain stocks. You can find a stock screener online on most financial websites. Why is this the first time we're mentioning it? Because we wanted you to know how to do all your proper research first!

Another thing to consider when looking for bargain stocks is that it doesn't pay to get too emotionally attached to them. When you buy your big-money, long-term stocks, it really is okay to purchase a few shares in a company you really enjoy the products from, but it is really important to remember that stocks are purely business. And when you purchase a share, you are purchasing a small piece of ownership in that company.

You should always have a business-like mindset when purchasing bargain stocks because you don't want to hold on to them too long if they are underperforming. That's why you want to have a cushion, and don't be afraid to sell your shares before your first dividend payout, if it seems that you'll be losing money by holding on to the stock that long.

Another good strategy for buying bargain stocks is to split up your investment funds and not spend them all at once. You can divide your market money in two, and purchase some shares of the stock now to see how the first dividend payout goes, and then use the other half to purchase more for the next dividend period. You could also split your money into three segments, and try your hand at three different stocks and then sell any that don't perform well. This is like a gardener who plants three seeds and then culls the two weaker seedlings to encourage the third, stronger seedling to grow.

The other thing you can do once you've set your bargain stock budget is to choose several stocks within the same sector, and invest small amounts in all of them. This is known as buying the basket. Once you've had time to see how the stocks perform over a dividend payout period, you can cut your losses and reinvest in the stocks that performed the best. When it comes to bargain stocks, don't waste time or money when it is clear that a stock is an underperformer. That may sound brutal, but stocks don't have feelings.

The last tip we can offer on choosing bargain stocks is to look at businesses in sectors that you understand. If you don't know what a business does or how it operates, it will be harder to put the metrics together. Numbers are wonderful tools, and as we said before, they don't lie, but knowing and understanding the business they are attached to will give you a greater sense of context as to what the numbers mean. This is important to the overall picture of why a company is performing as it is.

The final word on looking for value at your stock prices is to understand that, sometimes, the market dictates that there are no bargains. You shouldn't despair if you've done all your research and no good bargains really jump out at you. Spend your energy and your money elsewhere for a while, then look again. You'll be better off buying fewer shares of a stock with better returns and dividends than you would be buying a stock just for its low price and getting burned in the long-run.

A couple of chapters ago, we talked about moving and saving your dividend earnings to be used at a later date. But what if you want to use dividend payouts as your primary income? Is it possible to earn enough on dividends so that your returns become your regular finances? Let's take a look at some ways to live day-to-day off your earnings.

Chapter 9: Living off Your Options

Doesn't the prospect of living off your dividends sound just marvelous? It is possible, but you'll need to put a great deal of time and thought into choosing your dividends, investing at the right times, and deciding how much you'll need to live comfortably off your options.

All investors dream of a time when they can live off their earnings and leave the cares of the world behind. Yes, that sounds idyllic, and frankly, not very realistic. But if you keep your feet on the ground and your head out of the clouds, it is possible to craft a portfolio that will give you the income to lead the lifestyle you'd like to provide for yourself and your loved ones.

How Much Money is Enough Money?

If you answered, "it's never enough" to the title in this heading, you're probably ready to take some risks to make as much money as you possibly can. That's great! The whole point of investing in the stock market is to make money. But the truth is, we can't all become fabulously wealthy overnight, and so, you'll need to employ some strategies to build usable wealth using dividends.

can enjoy to the fullest. We've almost made it all the way through our journey to discover the power of dividend investing. In the last chapter, we'll tackle taxation - how taxes affect your dividend income and your savings, and how you can best invest your money to get the most out of it after taxes.

Chapter 10: Be Tax-Savvy

What was it that Benjamin Franklin said about death and taxes? Ah, yes, taxes are inevitable, and income tax laws don't exclude the money made on dividend stocks. Except in certain situations, of course, because there's nothing more fun that deciphering the tax code to make sure you pay the correct amount on your stock income. Because the tax implications of dividend investing have so many variables, we're going to go over the most common tax scenarios of dividend income. These are the basic rules that govern the taxes on most dividends. Let's start with a refresher on regular and qualified dividends and work our way up to the more complicated stuff.

Regular v. Qualified Dividends

When you buy, your dividends have as much an effect on the tax implications of your dividend income than any other factor. As we briefly discussed earlier in the book, there is a significant difference in the tax rate between a regular, or ordinary dividend, and a qualified dividend. As a refresher, a dividend becomes qualified when it meets the following criteria:

- The stock is issued by an American corporation or a foreign company that regularly trades on the U.S. markets.

- You have been the owner of a record for 60 or more days during the 121- day period that begins 60 days after the ex-dividend date. For example, if the dividend date is June 1, then you would have to purchase and hold the stock for 60 days between April 2 and July 31.

Regular dividend payouts are taxed at the same rate as the regular income you receive at your place of employment. That means that you could be taxed up to just shy of 40 percent depending on your income level. If you had purchased your dividend stocks in the correct time frame for those dividends to be qualified, you would only be taxed up to a maximum of 20 percent. That could be giant tax savings for you, leaving more money either in your pocket or to be put back into your investment account.

For example, if you earned $25,000 in regular dividends, you would be taxed at 12 percent, costing you $3,000. If that same dividend was qualified, you'd not be taxed at all, meaning that you'd have earned the entire $25,000.

Like all rules, there are exceptions, but you should always try to make sure you purchase your dividend stocks within the period necessary to have the payouts be as a qualified dividend and not an ordinary dividend. State tax laws vary, and you should consult a broker, accountant, or financial planner to be sure that you understand your state's tax laws. You don't want to be delinquent in any income taxes on either the state or federal level.

Then there remains the question of whether stock dividend payouts are taxed the same way as cash dividend payouts. If you take your dividend in the form of additional stock, you will not be taxed on that stock until such time as you sell it or take a cash dividend. If you take your dividend payment in cash but immediately use it to purchase more of the same stock, you will be taxed on the dividend as if you had kept the money.

Some companies offer what's known as a DRIP, or dividend reinvestment program. These programs don't have much impact on tax implications, but they can make it simpler to put your money back into the company by automatically reinvesting your dividend payout back into more shares. While you'll still have to pay income taxes on the dividend, you'll often be charged less per share for your reinvestment, you'll avoid high transaction fees because the company itself is selling you the shares (no middleman), and these programs fit right into your laddering plan for building income.

The downside to DRIPs is that the investors' freedom of choice is taken away until all stocks are sold. There's also the fact that the dividends are still taxed at their customary rates, and the shares are tied up without much liquidity.

Exploring Tax-Free Options

Much earlier, we very briefly touched upon the advantages and disadvantages of a Roth IRA. Here, we'll delve into what exactly this type of account is, and how it can be a near-perfect tax shelter for working Americans who wish to invest for long-term financial health.

A Roth IRA is not the same as a typical IRA, which is a more traditional form of retirement savings account. A Roth IRA functions more like a brokerage account, and you can use it to your advantage in a variety of ways. There are certain restrictions on a Roth IRA, but the restrictions are mitigated by the advantages the account can offer. It should be noted, this type of account is not a 'get rich quick' scheme, but should be seen as long-term wealth builder which can be used for many purposes, and even left as a legacy after the account owner passes away.

The premise of a Roth IRA is simple; you pay your regular income taxes, and then put the money, post-tax, into the account, where it cannot be taxed again. Why is this important? Because it means your money can sit and compound interest for as long as you want it to, without fear of being taxed on it annually.

The rules surrounding a Roth IRA are fairly simple. You can only contribute so much to the fund each year, and that cap is currently $6,000. You can take money equaling your contributions from your Roth IRA at any time, but if you've had the account for less than five years, you may be subject to penalties. After five years, you may withdraw money that came from contributions or earnings without fearing penalty if you meet the following criteria:

-You are over age 59.5.

-You are using the money (up to $10,000) to purchase a home.

-You need the money for an unexpected medical expense.

-You are arranging to pay yourself in regularly scheduled increments so that you may live off the income in your account.

- In the event of your death or disablement, the Roth Ira would become the property of your estate.

You may be wondering what all this talk of a Roth IRA has to do with dividend investing. The answer is everything. When you use a Roth IRA like a brokerage account, the money within is can be used for investing, and any dividends paid into the account are not subject to taxation, and dividend income does not count against your annual contribution cap. A Roth IRA is also exempt from any capital gains tax, and there is also no tax on interest. Roth IRAs are also fairly safe from inflation.

To summarize, a Roth IRA is a tax-advantageous account that you may want to talk to your broker or financial planner about. It's also possible to set up Roth IRAs on your own, but if you've never held one of these accounts before, you should take some time to familiarize yourself with the rules and ask for assistance if you need it. You don't want to risk making a mistake with such a powerful financial tool.

The one significant disadvantage to a Roth IRA is that is cannot be used as collateral in a loan. This is because the IRS would consider the collateral value to be a distribution from your account and therefore would tax you on that distribution at the appropriate rate.

The two other options for not paying taxes on dividends right away is to have them deposited directly into your regular IRA or your 401(k) retirement fund. In these instances, you do not have to pay taxes until you begin drawing money from these types of funds.

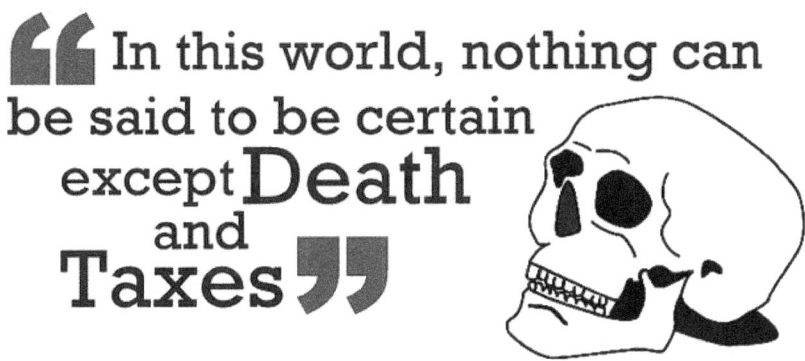

In this world, nothing can be said to be certain except Death and Taxes

Benjamin Franklin, Excerpt from a letter to Jean-Baptiste Leroy

- Franklin may have had it right!-

Franklin's Other Option

Remember how we opened this chapter with a hint of Benjamin Franklin's famous quote? Well, even in death, someone must carry on the family finances, and in the event of your death, your family would inherit your stock market accounts. If they choose to sell the assets, the proceeds would be taxed at the lower capital gains rate, like qualified dividends. Inherited stock is usually below the level that would indicate the need to pay a federal estate tax, but you should check to see if your state or the state(s) where your heirs reside have an estate or inheritance tax that may need to be paid.

If your family inherits your Roth IRA, they will not be charged taxes when they choose to take a distribution from the fund, because you paid taxes on the contributions before you made them. But seriously, death isn't the best option for avoiding taxes. There are plenty of ways to be tax-savvy without going to the great beyond.

On a happier note, if you choose to donate to a charitable foundation or non-profit by transferring stocks to them as an asset, neither you nor the group receiving the stock will have to pay income or capital gains tax on them. A direct transfer can be a bit of a paperwork jam, but you can put the assets you wish to donate into a *donor-advised fund* (DAF), which will take a lot of the guesswork out of contributing assets to charity. You can start a DAF online by yourself, or ask your broker for advice on how to set one up. As an added bonus, you will receive a tax deduction for your charitable donations.

Taxes on Foreign Investments

When you make the move to add foreign investments to your portfolio, you need to be aware of the tax implications, which we briefly touched upon in Chapter 5. Some experts say that when you diversify your portfolio, you should be looking to add up to 30 percent foreign stocks, which can really boost your income but also affect your taxes.

You need to know that you will be taxed on your dividends accordingly in the United States, at whatever the appropriate rate is. But you will also be taxed according to the tax laws of the country where your dividend originated. Some countries waive the income tax for foreign investors, but some, like Italy for example, charge up to 20 percent. You need to be cognizant of these tax rates when you're deciding to choose foreign stocks.

Take heart, though, it's not all bad news. There's a tax credit offered by the IRS for foreign investment income, and it's called, very creatively, the Foreign Tax Credit. What this means for your bottom line is that you will be able to offset some or all of the foreign tax using the credit when you file your taxes.

Foreign Tax Paid	$300
U.S. Tax Liability	$200
Foreign Tax Credit	**$200**
Carryover Amount	**$100**

- An example of how the Foreign Tax Credit can reduce some of your tax burdens-

Final Thoughts on Taxes

As we near the end of our chapter and the end of this book, let's take a moment to be serious about taxes. Pay them *when they arise.* There is no foolproof way to avoid paying taxes, and you'll be far better off giving the government a little money now than paying hefty fines and penalties later. Or the worst-case scenario, being charged with tax fraud and potentially facing trial, criminal consequences, and/or jail time.

If you have any questions about taxes, use a certified public accountant or tax specialist, and don't hesitate to ask them about anything you are unsure of. Tax laws are complicated and only continue to get more so. You want to make sure you know everything you need to know about the tax implications of your investments to avoid any trouble. It's always better to ask now than find out once it is too late. You don't want to make any costly mistakes when it comes to filing your taxes.

As certain as Franklin was about death and taxes, it is as certain as you should now be in your ability to begin placing your investments confidently in dividend stocks. We've reached the end of the book, but this is only the beginning of your life as a dividend investor.

Conclusion

And now, we've reached the end of our dividend investing journey together. Thank you again for taking the time to purchase and read *Dividend Investing: A Complete Step-by-Step Beginners Guide to Dominate the Stock Market and Build Your Own Passive Income Toward Financial Freedom with Investing in Dividend Stocks*. We hope you've enjoyed the read, and that it was beneficial in answering all your basic dividend investing questions.

With the information in this book, you should now be well on your way to getting started with dividend stocks. The key points to take away from these lessons are that doing your research is always crucial, and knowing how to read the market is an important step in being a successful investor. We've also pushed the importance of patience and pragmatism. These values will carry you far in the world of dividend investing.

We also covered a great deal of material about using your dividend stocks to increase your wealth through savings and reinvestment. The wonderful thing about dividend stocks is that they are a stable, relatively low-risk way to increase your income, but you do need to remember the lessons on being patient. Speculative trading is a sprint, but dividend investing is a marathon, and you want to give yourself the tools to cross the finish line.

You can read this book once and feel confident in knowing that you've got all the basic knowledge you need to begin investing in dividend stocks. You can also use this book as a reference for when you're feeling uncertain or need a refresher. There are also a lot of topics in this book that can spawn curiosity, and we hope you'll take the initiative to further investigate anything that interests you or that you'd like more information about.

The stock market can seem like a daunting and complicated financial institution, but it's not the exclusive old-money club it once was, nor is it the wildly volatile scene it was during the industrial boom that led to the Great Depression. The stock market truly is for everyone these days, and with the cost of living soaring, what better way is there to make some extra income for yourself than by investing in stocks that pay you back?

Dividend investing can allow you financial freedom, some breathing room on expenses, and give you and your family income with which to live life more fully. It can also help you fund major purchases, pay for education, and set aside a nest egg to help you through your retirement years. In today's fast-paced society, making investments that mature slowly may be the best thing you can do for yourself and your financial health.

We're so grateful you chose to read *Dividend Investing: A Complete Step-by-Step Beginners Guide to Dominate the Stock Market and Build Your Own Passive Income Toward Financial Freedom with Investing in Dividend Stocks.*

Good luck and happy investing! May all your financial goals come true.

www.ingramcontent.com/pod-product-compliance
Lightning Source LLC
Chambersburg PA
CBHW070356220526
45467CB00001B/399